# Yocto for Raspberry Pi

Create unique and amazing projects by using the
powerful combination of Yocto and Raspberry Pi

**Pierre-Jean Texier**
**Petter Mabäcker**

BIRMINGHAM - MUMBAI

# Yocto for Raspberry Pi

First published: June 2016

Production reference: 1170616

Published by Packt Publishing Ltd.
Livery Place
35 Livery Street
Birmingham
B3 2PB, UK.
ISBN 978-1-78528-195-2

www.packtpub.com

# Credits

**Authors**
Pierre-Jean TEXIER
Petter Mabäcker

**Reviewers**
Burt Janz
Dave (Jing) Tian
Helmi ROMDHANI
Pierre FICHEUX

**Commissioning Editor**
Amarabha Banerjee

**Acquisition Editor**
Meeta Rajani

**Content Development Editor**
Rashmi Suvarna

**Technical Editor**
Mohit Hassija

**Copy Editor**
Madhusudan Uchil

**Project Coordinator**
Judie Jose

**Proofreader**
Safis Editing

**Indexer**
Hemangini Bari

**Production Coordinator**
Shantanu N. Zagade

**Cover Work**
Shantanu N. Zagade

# About the Authors

**Pierre-Jean TEXIER** is an embedded Linux engineer at Amplitude Systèmes (a pioneer in the marketing of Ytterbium femtosecond lasers) since 2014, where he maintains a custom SoC called i.MX6 with the Yocto Project (meta-fsl-arm), which is made by a French company, EUKREA.

He is a graduate of ESTEI school at Bordeaux, where he studied for 3 years to become an embedded Linux engineer.

He is a big supporter of the world of free software and the embedded world. His knowledge includes C/C++, Yocto, Linux, Bash, and kernel development, but he is also open to trying new things and testing new technologies.

*Firstly, I want to thank my patient wife for her support during my writing sessions. I also give thanks my parents and my brother; without them, this book possibly would not have happened. I would also like to thank all of the mentors that I've had over the years—mentors such as Cyril SAGONERO, Sylvain LE HENAFF, Pierre BORDELAIS, Vincent POULAILLEAU, Fabrice BONNET, Jean-Claude PERESSINOTTO, and Pierre AUBRY. Without learning from these teachers, there is not a chance I could be doing what I do today. To finish, I would like to thank Eric MOTTAY, the CEO of Amplitude Systèmes; Luca TESTA, the head of the electronics team at Amplitude Systèmes for his trust; and Hitesham WOODHOO, Alexandre GAMONET, Kevin PINTO, and Guillaume MACHINET for all the discussions about the Raspberry Pi during coffee breaks.*

**Petter Mabäcker** is a senior software developer specializing in embedded Linux systems. For the past 8 years, he has been working with embedded Linux professionally. Currently, Petter works as a Scrum Master and senior software developer at Ericsson AB. Additionally, his knowledge includes C/C++, shell scripting, Yocto Project (including BitBake and OpenEmbedded), Scrum, and Git.

In 2013, Petter started the small business Technux, which he runs as a side project in parallel with his duties at Ericsson. Some of the focus areas of the business are open source embedded Linux projects, such as the Yocto Project, together with different projects that involve the Raspberry Pi. As part of the work with Technux, Petter works as a contributer to the Yocto Project (including the Raspberry Pi BSP layer, known as meta-raspberrypi ).

*I would like to give special thanks to my beloved family for letting me spend the time needed to finalize this book besides all my other duties.*

# About the Reviewers

**Burt Janz** has been involved with computing systems since he assembled his first microcomputer in the US Navy in 1975. Starting with the development of device drivers and low-level interfaces on *nix systems in the early 1980s, Mr. Janz has been writing complex software products for over 30 years. His expertise stretches from the design and implementation of low-level operating system internals and device drivers to complex applications for embedded and handheld devices and government and enterprise-level systems.

A 1988 graduate with high honors in BSCS from Franklin Pierce College, he was an adjunct professor at Daniel Webster College for 11 years in their evening-based Continuing Education program, developing embedded and enterprise-level software during the day. His curricula of instruction included courses from a basic introduction to computers to programming languages (C/C++/Java) to networking theory and network programming, database theory and schema design, artificial intelligence systems. Along the way, Mr. Janz has written magazine articles and other technical commentaries as well as having been involved with one of the first over-the-counter Linux distributions (Yggdrasil, in 1994).

Mr. Janz has designed complete embedded and enterprise-level software system architectures as a lead architect and has led teams from the requirements and design phases of new products through to completion and delivery to customers. He has experience with x86, 68xxx, PPC, ARM, and SPARC processors and continues to write kernel threads and kmods, open firmware device trees, drivers for new and proprietary hardware, FPGA I/P core interfaces, applications, libraries, and boot manager code. He may be contacted directly by email at bhjanz@ccsneinc.com or burt.janz@gmail.com or via LinkedIn.

**Dave (Jing) Tian** is a PhD student and a security researcher at the Computer & Information Science & Engineering (CISE) department of the University of Florida. He is a founding member of the SENSEI center and the Florida Institute for Cybersecurity. His research involves system security, embedded systems, trusted computing, and compilers. He has an interest in Linux kernel hacking, compiler hacking, and machine learning. He also spent a year on AI and machine learning direction and taught Python and operating system classes at the University of Oregon. Before that, he worked as a software developer at the Linux Control Platform (LCP) group at Alcatel-Lucent (former Lucent Technologies) R&D department for around 4 years. He holds BS and ME degrees in EE from China. He can be reached via his blog (http://davejingtian.org) and e-mail (root@davejingtian.org).

Thanks to the authors, who have done a good job, and the editors, who made this book perfect and offered me the opportunity to review such a nice book.

**Helmi ROMDHANI** is an embedded HW/SW engineer. He graduated from the national engineering school of Sousse, Tunisia. His primary job is at Tunisian Embedded Systems, which specializes in the research, development, prototyping, and installation of embedded systems. He specializes in embedded telecommunication field, especially in developing embedded software for residential gateways. He frequently works with embedded platforms (Raspberry Pi and Arduino), Linux, shell, Yocto, Python, C# (.Net), Android, databases (MySQL), web services, and Proteus Isis (PCB design).

Any contact is welcome at `helmiromdhany@gmail.com`.

I would like to thank all my family for their support, encouragement, and love, especially my mother, Salha, and my father, Mokhtar.

**Pierre FICHEUX** is currently the CTO at Open Wide Ingénierie, a software service company specializing in open source technologies.

Pierre is also a teacher and manager of the GISTRE (Génie Informatique des Systèmes Temps Réel et Embarqués) specialty at EPITA, a famous French school of computer science.

He's also an author of four editions of Linux Embarqué, Eyrolles , a French reference book about building embedded Linux systems.

# www.PacktPub.com

## eBooks, discount offers, and more

Did you know that Packt offers eBook versions of every book published, with PDF and ePub files available? You can upgrade to the eBook version at www.PacktPub.com and as a print book customer, you are entitled to a discount on the eBook copy. Get in touch with us at customercare@packtpub.com for more details.

At www.PacktPub.com, you can also read a collection of free technical articles, sign up for a range of free newsletters and receive exclusive discounts and offers on Packt books and eBooks.

https://www2.packtpub.com/books/subscription/packtlib

Do you need instant solutions to your IT questions? PacktLib is Packt's online digital book library. Here, you can search, access, and read Packt's entire library of books.

## Why subscribe?

- Fully searchable across every book published by Packt
- Copy and paste, print, and bookmark content
- On demand and accessible via a web browser

# Table of Contents

**Preface**                                                                    1

**Chapter 1: Meeting the Yocto Project**                                        7

  **The Yocto Project**                                               7
    Understanding the build system                           8
  **The core components**                                             10
    What is Poky?                                           11
    The Chief – BitBake                                     12
    OpenEmbedded-Core                                       14
    Exploring metadata                                      16
  **Yocto Project – workflow**                                        17
  **Summary**                                                         18

**Chapter 2: Building our First Poky Image for the Raspberry Pi**              19

  **Installing the required packages for the host system**            19
    Poky on Ubuntu                                          20
    Poky on Fedora                                          21
    Downloading the Poky metadata                           21
    Downloading the Raspberry Pi BSP metadata               22
    The oe-init-build-env script                            25
    Editing the local.conf file                             26
    Editing the bblayers.conf file                          26
  **Building the Poky image**                                         27
    Choice of image                                         27
    Running BitBake                                         29
    Creating an SD card                                     30
  **Booting the image on the Raspberry Pi**                           31
  **Summary**                                                         32

**Chapter 3: Mastering Baking with Hob and Toaster**                           33

  **Hob**                                                             33
    Preparing the environment for Hob                       33
    Running Hob                                             34
    Configuring recipes and packages                        40
    Building the image                                      42
  **Exploring Toaster**                                               44

| | |
|---|---|
| Installing the required packages for the host system | 44 |
| Running Toaster | 44 |
| Running BitBake | 45 |
| Running the web interface | 46 |
| **Summary** | 46 |
| **Chapter 4: Understanding BitBake** | 47 |
| **BitBake** | 47 |
| **Metadata** | 48 |
| Configuration | 48 |
| Classes | 48 |
| Recipes | 49 |
| **Parsing metadata** | 49 |
| **Preferences and providers** | 50 |
| **Dependencies** | 50 |
| **Fetching** | 51 |
| The local file fetcher | 51 |
| The HTTP fetcher | 52 |
| The Git fetcher | 52 |
| **Understanding BitBake's tasks** | 53 |
| **Summary** | 55 |
| **Chapter 5: Creating, Developing, and Deploying on the Raspberry Pi** | 57 |
| **Software development kits (SDKs)** | 57 |
| A generic SDK – meta-toolchain | 59 |
| image.bb -c populate_sdk | 59 |
| The Qt SDK – meta-toolchain-qt | 60 |
| The Qt5 SDK – meta-toolchain-qt5 | 61 |
| Cross-compilation – an example | 61 |
| Configuration of the SDK environment | 61 |
| List of tools | 62 |
| Compilation | 62 |
| **Raspberry Pi and a package manager** | 63 |
| Package format availablility | 63 |
| Choosing a package format | 64 |
| Installing and updating a package on the target | 65 |
| RPM packages | 65 |
| Installing manually | 65 |
| Installing automatically | 65 |
| IPK packages | 68 |
| Installing manually | 68 |

| | |
|---|---|
| Installing automatically | 68 |
| **Our application – an introduction** | 69 |
| **Our application – creating the recipe** | 71 |
| The recipe explained | 72 |
| **Summary** | 74 |
| **Chapter 6: Working with External Layers** | **75** |
| **Introducing layers** | 75 |
| **The basic concepts of layers** | 76 |
| Theory | 76 |
| The software layer | 78 |
| README and COPYING | 78 |
| The classes folder | 79 |
| The conf folder | 79 |
| The recipes-* directory | 80 |
| The machine (BSP) layer | 80 |
| **Adding external layers to the Raspberry Pi** | 82 |
| **Summary** | 83 |
| **Chapter 7: Deploying a Custom Layer on the Raspberry Pi** | **85** |
| **Creating the meta-packt_rpi layer with the yocto-layer script** | 85 |
| **Adding gpio-packt to meta-packt_rpi** | 88 |
| **Patching gpio-packt** | 90 |
| Generating the patch | 90 |
| Adding the patch to the recipe file | 90 |
| **Creating the raspberry-packt-image.bb image** | 92 |
| Creating the environment | 92 |
| Modifying the recipe file | 93 |
| **Deploying the raspberry-packt-image.bb image** | 95 |
| **Summary** | 95 |
| **Chapter 8: Diving into the Raspberry Pi's Peripherals and Yocto Recipes** | **97** |
| **The SPI bus** | 97 |
| The spi-tools project | 98 |
| Inclusion in the meta-oe layer | 99 |
| Baking spi-tools | 100 |
| Testing on the Raspberry Pi | 101 |
| spi-config | 101 |
| spi-pipe | 102 |
| Conclusion | 103 |
| **The i2c bus** | 103 |

**The Wii Nunchuck**     105
The Nunchuck connector     106
**The Raspberry Pi connection**     107
The Nunchuck's protocol     107
    Encryption     108
    Requesting sensor data     108
Testing the i2c connection     109
Creating the Nunchuck application     110
Integrating with meta-packt_rpi     110
Creating the Nunchuck recipe     111
Testing the Nunchuck application     112
V4L presentation     112
Video support     112
v4l-utils integration     113
**Summary**     114

**Chapter 9: Making a Media Hub on the Raspberry Pi**     115
**Project description – CPU temperature monitoring**     115
Overview     116
Hardware/software requirements     116
**Creating the main application**     116
server.js     117
index.html     117
**Creating the Yocto/OE environment**     118
Modifying the image     118
Creating the recipe file     118
    Explanation     120
Autostarting – the init file     121
    Explanation     122
Autostarting – the recipe file     123
Explanation     124
**Deploying raspberry-packt-image**     124
**Testing the application**     125
**The future of this project**     126
**Summary**     126

**Chapter 10: Playing with an LCD Touchscreen and the Linux Kernel**     127
**The Linux kernel**     127
The Linux kernels versus the Raspberry Pi Linux kernel     128
Getting started with the Linux kernel     129
    Configuring the kernel in Yocto     132

Configuring the kernel with LCD support                                              133
   The Raspberry Pi device tree                                        134
   Configuring the touchscreen from the kernel perspective             135
**Setting up an LCD display for the Raspberry Pi using the Yocto
Project**                                                                            137
   The Raspberry Pi 7 touchscreen                                      137
   The PiTFT 2.8 resistive touchscreen                                 139
**Developing applications and using them on an LCD display**                         141
   Developing a custom application using Qt                            142
**Summary**                                                                          145

**Chapter 11: Contributing to the Raspberry Pi BSP Layer**                           147

**Open source**                                                                      147
**Contributing to open source projects**                                             148
**Exploring Git**                                                                    148
   What is Git?                                                        149
   Working with Git                                                    149
**Contributing to the Yocto Project**                                                155
   Contributing to meta-raspberrypi                                    156
     Setting up your Git repository                          157
   Creating your commit                                               158
   Sending changes to the community                                    160
   Follow-up                                                           161
   Practical example – sending a custom tool upstream                  162
**Summary**                                                                          164

**Chapter 12: Home Automation Project - Booting a Custom Image**                     165

**Home automation using a Raspberry Pi**                                             165
   Material required for the project                                   166
**Setting up the base for the project**                                              167
   Creating a new layer                                                167
   Customizing the image recipe                                        167
   Building and booting the image                                      168
**Creating the server side**                                                         171
**Creating a packet list for your image**                                            178
   Setting up a customized package list                                178
   Start using a customized package list in meta-packt-iot             179
**Putting it all together**                                                          180
     Serial and SSH connections to the Raspberry Pi          180
   Controlling the relay using the Raspberry Pi                        183
   Controlling the lamp using the Raspberry Pi                         186

| | |
|---|---|
| Turning on/off the lamp from a smartphone | 189 |
| **Extra – using a Raspberry Pi with an LCD as the client** | 190 |
| **Summary** | 192 |
| **Index** | 193 |

# Preface

This book will cover everything from creating your customized image for the Raspberry Pi to implementing a small home automation project using the Yocto Project and the Raspberry Pi as the base.

The book will start by introducing you to the Yocto Project and presenting the Raspberry Pi platform. With this information in place, you will learn how to integrate the Yocto Project with the Raspberry Pi. Throughout the book, you will learn everything from how to develop a custom application to using a Wii nunchuck and configuring an LCD touchscreen for the Raspberry Pi using the Yocto Project. The book will end with a practical chapter, which will summarize all that you learned throughout the book by creating a home automation project.

## What this book covers

Chapter 1, *Meeting the Yocto Project*, introduces the basic concept of the Yocto Project. It will discuss history of the Yocto Project, OpenEmbedded Core, Poky, and BitBake.

Chapter 2, *Building our First Poky Image for the Raspberry Pi*, teaches you how to create your first image for the Raspberry Pi using the Yocto Project and how to run it.

Chapter 3, *Mastering Baking with Hob and Toaster*, teaches you how to use the user-friendly interfaces Hob and Toaster.

Chapter 4, *Understanding BitBake*, provides you with a deeper understanding of BitBake.

Chapter 5, *Creating, Developing, and Deploying on the Raspberry Pi,* teaches you how to integrate a custom application with the Raspberry Pi. This will include learning how to generate an SDK for cross-compiling applications.

Chapter 6, *Working with External Layers*, takes you through how layers work and how to integrate external layers with our Raspberry Pi projects.

Chapter 7, *Deploying a Custom Layer on the Raspberry Pi*, explores how to generate a custom layer with different tools that the Yocto Project offers.

Chapter 8, *Diving into the Raspberry Pi's Peripherals and Yocto Recipes*, teaches you how to handle the SPI and i2C buses of the Raspberry Pi through the Yocto Project. You will also learn how to create your own recipe for custom applications.

Chapter 9, *Making a Media Hub on the Raspberry Pi*, goes through how to deploy custom applications in order to make an embedded media hub, which can be used to, for example, monitor CPU temperature. The solution will require HTML5 and Node.js to set up the web interface required for remotely monitoring temperature.

Chapter 10, *Playing with an LCD Touchscreen and the Linux Kernel*, teaches you some basics about the Linux kernel and how to configure it to support various LCD touchscreens. Further on, the chapter explains how to set up the Yocto Project to run graphical applications or a window system on a Raspberry Pi using an LCD touchscreen.

Chapter 11, *Contributing to the Raspberry Pi BSP Layer*, teaches you how to contribute to the meta-raspberrypi layer.

Chapter 12, *Home Automation Project – Booting a Custom Image*, is the final chapter of the book, in which we summarize all that we learned throughout the book. This is done by creating a home automation project.

# What you need for this book

- A Linux workstation with a supported host system (see `http://www.yoctoproj ect.org/docs/current/ref-manual/ref-manual.html#detailed-suppor ted-distros`)
- Packages required for the host system (see `http://www.yoctoproject.org/do cs/current/ref-manual/ref-manual.html#required-packages-for-the -host-development-system`)
- The required versions of Git, tar, and Python (see `http://www.yoctoproject. org/docs/current/ref-manual/ref-manual.html#required-git-tar-an d-python-versions`)

# Who this book is for

This book is intended for embedded software students, embedded Linux engineers, and embedded systems enthusiasts competent with the Raspberry Pi (or another ARM platform) who want to discover the Yocto Project.

This book is the ideal way to become proficient and broaden your knowledge in order to apply it to your embedded development.

If you are looking for a book to help you develop on the Raspberry Pi and the Yocto Project, this book is the one you need.

# Conventions

In this book, you will find a number of text styles that distinguish between different kinds of information. Here are some examples of these styles and an explanation of their meaning.

Code words in text, database table names, folder names, filenames, file extensions, path names, dummy URLs, user input, and Twitter handles are shown as follows: "To run a task, BitBake will first look for an environment variable called do_ <task name>, which will contain the task code to execute (in Python or a shell)."

A block of code is set as follows:

```
# LAYER_CONF_VERSION is increased each time build/conf/bblayers.conf
# changes incompatibly
LCONF_VERSION = "6" BBPATH = "${TOPDIR}" BBFILES ?= "" BBLAYERS ?= " \
/home/packt/RASPBERRYPI/poky/meta \
/home/packt/RASPBERRYPI/poky/meta-yocto \
/home/packt/RASPBERRYPI/poky/meta-yocto-bsp \
"BBLAYERS_NON_REMOVABLE ?= " \
/home/packt/RASPBERRYPI/poky/meta \
/home/packt/RASPBERRYPI/poky/meta-yocto \
"
```

Any command-line input or output is written as follows:

```
$ modprobe spidev
```

**New terms** and **important words** are shown in bold. Words that you see on the screen, for example, in menus or dialog boxes, appear in the text like this: "Adding a layer is very simple. We just have to click on the **Layers** button."

Warnings or important notes appear in a box like this.

Tips and tricks appear like this.

# Reader feedback

Feedback from our readers is always welcome. Let us know what you think about this book-what you liked or disliked. Reader feedback is important for us as it helps us develop titles that you will really get the most out of. To send us general feedback, simply e-mail feedback@packtpub.com, and mention the book's title in the subject of your message. If there is a topic that you have expertise in and you are interested in either writing or contributing to a book, see our author guide at www.packtpub.com/authors.

# Customer support

Now that you are the proud owner of a Packt book, we have a number of things to help you to get the most from your purchase.

# Downloading the example code

You can download the example code files for this book from your account at http://www.packtpub.com. If you purchased this book elsewhere, you can visit http://www.packtpub.com/support and register to have the files e-mailed directly to you.

You can download the code files by following these steps:

1. Log in or register to our website using your e-mail address and password.
2. Hover the mouse pointer on the **SUPPORT** tab at the top.
3. Click on **Code Downloads & Errata**.
4. Enter the name of the book in the **Search** box.
5. Select the book for which you're looking to download the code files.
6. Choose from the drop-down menu where you purchased this book from.
7. Click on **Code Download**.

Once the file is downloaded, please make sure that you unzip or extract the folder using the latest version of:

- WinRAR / 7-Zip for Windows
- Zipeg / iZip / UnRarX for Mac
- 7-Zip / PeaZip for Linux

The code bundle for the book is also hosted on GitHub at `https://github.com/PacktPu blishing/Yocto-for-Raspberry-Pi`. We also have other code bundles from our rich catalog of books and videos available at `https://github.com/PacktPublishing/`. Check them out!

# Downloading the color images of this book

We also provide you with a PDF file that has color images of the screenshots/diagrams used in this book. The color images will help you better understand the changes in the output. You can download this file from `https://www.packtpub.com/sites/default/files/ downloads/YoctoforRaspberryPi_ColorImages.pdf`.

# Errata

Although we have taken every care to ensure the accuracy of our content, mistakes do happen. If you find a mistake in one of our books-maybe a mistake in the text or the code-we would be grateful if you could report this to us. By doing so, you can save other readers from frustration and help us improve subsequent versions of this book. If you find any errata, please report them by visiting `http://www.packtpub.com/submit-errata`, selecting your book, clicking on the **Errata Submission Form** link, and entering the details of your errata. Once your errata are verified, your submission will be accepted and the errata will be uploaded to our website or added to any list of existing errata under the Errata section of that title.

To view the previously submitted errata, go to `https://www.packtpub.com/books/content/support` and enter the name of the book in the search field. The required information will appear under the **Errata** section.

# Piracy

Piracy of copyrighted material on the Internet is an ongoing problem across all media. At Packt, we take the protection of our copyright and licenses very seriously. If you come across any illegal copies of our works in any form on the Internet, please provide us with the location address or website name immediately so that we can pursue a remedy.

Please contact us at `copyright@packtpub.com` with a link to the suspected pirated material.

We appreciate your help in protecting our authors and our ability to bring you valuable content.

# Questions

If you have a problem with any aspect of this book, you can contact us at `questions@packtpub.com`, and we will do our best to address the problem.

# 1

# Meeting the Yocto Project

In this chapter, we will discover the Yocto Project and its main principles. All the concepts used throughout the book will be introduced here. We will discuss the history of the Yocto Project, the build system, Poky, OpenEmbedded-Core, BitBake, metadata, and the Yocto Project workflow.

## The Yocto Project

The Yocto Project is an umbrella project covering a fairly wide gamut of embedded Linux technologies. It is *not* a Linux distribution, as explained on the Yocto Project website:

*"The Yocto Project is an open source collaboration project that provides templates, tools and methods to help you create custom Linux-based systems for embedded products regardless of the hardware architecture."*

Sponsored by the Linux Foundation, the Yocto Project is more than a build system. It provides tools, processes, templates and methods so that developers can rapidly create and deploy products for embedded devices(the Raspberry Pi, Beagleboard, Nitrogen6x, SAMA5D3, Olinuxino, and so on) or QEMU. The two main components that make up the Yocto Project are:

- Poky: This is the build system (the reference distribution).
- BitBake: This is the scheduler. It is a tool based on the Gentoo distribution.

Around November 2010, the Linux Foundation announced that this entire work would continue under the banner of the Yocto Project as a project sponsored by the Linux Foundation (with Richard Purdie, Fellow of the Linux Foundation, as Architect). It was then established that the Yocto Project and OpenEmbedded would coordinate on a core set of package metadata called **OE-Core**, combining the best of both Poky and OpenEmbedded with an increased use of layering for additional components.

# Understanding the build system

As mentioned before, we are in the world of build systems with the Yocto Project. A build system enables you to:

- Compile or cross-compile applications
- Package applications
- Test output binaries and ecosystem compatibility
- Deploy generated images

To perform these steps, several tools exist. These are some of them:

- Buildroot (http://buildroot.uclibc.org/)
- LTIB (http://ltib.org/)
- OpenWRT (https://openwrt.org/)
- Yocto/OpenEmbedded (https://www.yoctoproject.org/)

For example, Buildroot is a set of makefiles for automated generation in embedded systems. It supports compiling the bootloader (U-Boot, for example), kernel (zImage or bzImage), and basic controls through BusyBox and third-party applications. Buildroot works on various architectures, such as ARM, x86, and MIPS. For further information, refer to the full documentation in English at `https://buildroot.org/docs.html`.

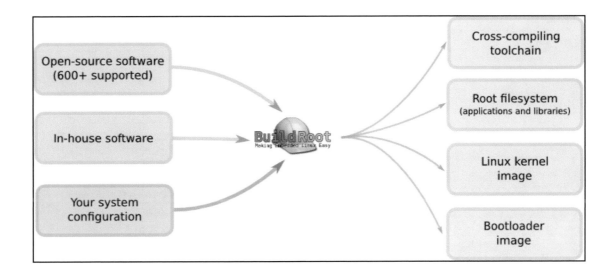

*"Buildroot is a tool maintained in part by a French company that specializes in embedded Linux development called Free Electrons"*

Buildroot is a much more simplistic approach than the one we will discover through this book on the Yocto Project. Buildroot is rather dedicated to *firmware* generation, while Yocto/OpenEmbedded is oriented towards *distribution*. Buildroot offers 700 recipes compared to the Yocto Project, which offers over 8000.

# The core components

The core components (other available tools are optional) of the Yocto Project are:

- BitBake
- OpenEmbedded-Core
- Poky
- The BSP layer (meta-raspberry, meta-fsl-arm, meta-ti, meta-intel, meta-sunxi, and so on)

The following diagram shows all the layers that we will discover through this book. We will study all the tools through various examples, allowing better comprehension.

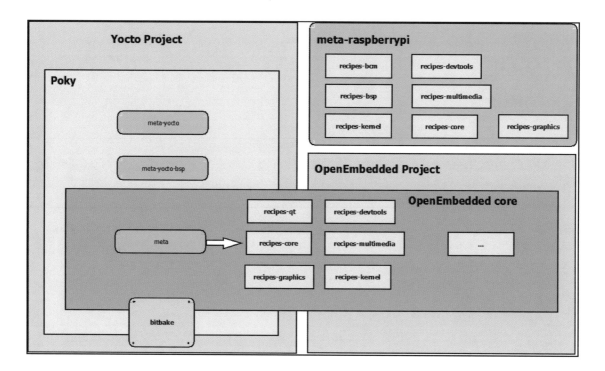

# What is Poky?

**Poky** is the *reference* Yocto Project distribution. It contains some of basic components (called the build system) of OpenEmbedded and a set of metadata for creating embedded distributions for a number of targets. It is platform independent and performs cross-compiling using the BitBake tool (a task scheduler), OpenEmbedded-Core, and a default set of metadata, as shown in the following figure. It provides the mechanism to build and combine thousands of distributed open source projects.

The Poky build system is poised to become the reference in the industrial world as evinces by industry leaders such as Wind River, Intel, Montavista, and Mentor Graphics.

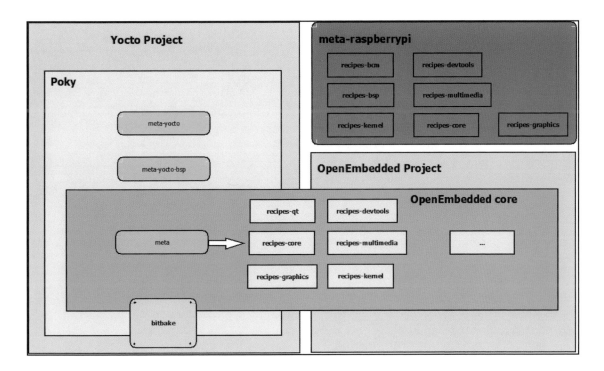

Angstrom (`http://www.angstrom-distribution.org/`) is another distribution based on OpenEmbedded-Core. You might consider Angstrom and Poky to be close cousins, because Poky is also based on OpenEmbedded-Core.

# The Chief – BitBake

**BitBake**, the build engine, is a task scheduler (like GNU Make) which parses several scripts (shell and Python, for example).

Once the environment is built, BitBake will execute the task that has been requested. If no task is provided, BitBake will run the default task, called `build`.

To run a task, BitBake will first look for an environment variable called `do_ <task name>`, which will contain the task code to execute (in Python or a shell). So, to compile a Yocto recipe, use the code contained in the `do_compile` variable.

In short, from the information contained in the recipes (or **metadata**), it downloads the sources of projects from the Internet, a local directory, or a version-control system (such as **Git**), and then builds in the order determined by the dependency graph generated dynamically. Finally, it installs binaries, generates the corresponding package, and builds the final image, which can be installed on the target (Raspberry Pi for us).

The following picture shows how BitBake works:

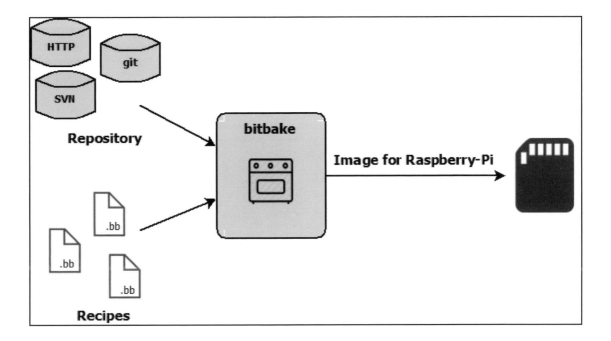

# OpenEmbedded-Core

The OpenEmbedded-Core metadata collection (**meta** in the following diagram) provides the engine of the Poky build tool. It is designed to provide the core features (several recipes). It provides support for six different processor architectures (ARM, x86, x86-64, PowerPC, MIPS, and MIPS64), supporting only QEMU-emulated machines.

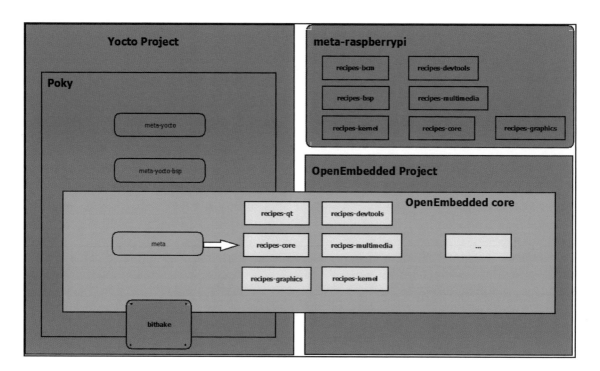

The organization of OpenEmbedded-Core is depicted here:

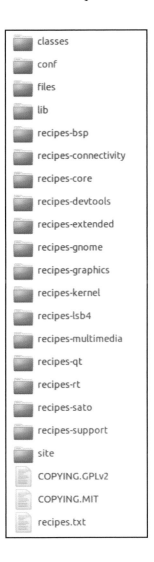

This layer includes different recipes, which describe how to fetch, configure, compile and package applications and images.

 For the rest of the book, we will mix this layer with the BSP layer of the Raspberry Pi, **meta-raspberrypi**.

# Exploring metadata

**Metadata**, which is composed of a mix of Python and shell script text files (`.conf`, `.bb`, `.bbclass`, and `.inc`), provides a tremendously flexible system. Metadata refers to the build instructions themselves as well as the data used to control what things get built and to affect how they are built. The metadata also includes commands and data used to indicate which versions of software are used and where they are obtained from. Poky uses this to extend OpenEmbedded-Core and includes two different layers, which are another metadata subset. Here are their details:

- * **meta-yocto**: This layer provides the default and supported distributions, visual branding, and metadata tracking information (maintainers, upstream status, and so on)
- * **meta-yocto-bsp**: This layer, on top of it, provides the hardware reference board support (BSP) for use in Poky

We will discover metadata in depth through Chapter 4, *Understanding the BitBake tool*.

# Yocto Project – workflow

The following diagram represents the Yocto Project development environment at a high level in order to present the cross-compilation framework:

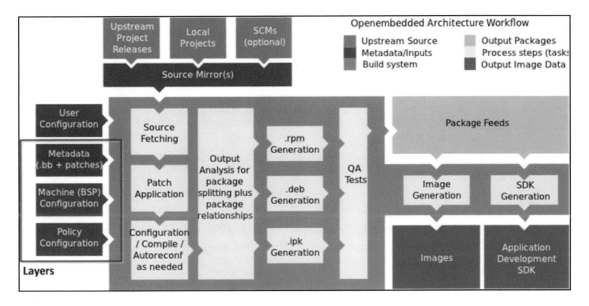

Let's look at what the components in the diagram stand for:

- * **User Configuration**: This is metadata you can use to control the build process.
- * **Metadata layers**: These are various layers that provide software, machine, and distribution metadata.
- * **Source files**: These contain upstream releases, local projects, and source control management (Git, SVN, and so on).

- * **Build system**: These are processes under the control of BitBake. This block expands on how BitBake fetches source files, applies patches, completes compilation, analyzes output for package generation, creates and tests packages, generates images, and generates cross-development tools.
- * **Package feeds**: These are directories containing output packages (RPM, DEB, or IPK), which are subsequently used in the construction of an image or SDK produced by the build system. These feeds can also be copied and shared using a web server or other means to facilitate extending or updating existing images on devices at runtime if runtime package management is enabled.
- * **Images**: These are images produced by the development process (the pieces that compose the operating system, such as the kernel image, bootloader, and rootfs).
- * **Application development SDK**: These are cross-development tools that are produced along with an image or separately with BitBake.

# Summary

This first chapter provided an overview on how the Yocto Project works, the core components that form it, such as Poky, OpenEmbedded-Core, and BitBake, and how they work within the Yocto Project.

In the next chapter, we will practice the workflow of the Yocto Project with different steps to download, configure, and prepare the Poky build environment in order to generate our first Poky image for the Raspberry Pi.

# 2
# Building our First Poky Image for the Raspberry Pi

In this chapter, we will try to understand the basic concepts of the Poky workflow. Using the Linux command line, we will proceed with the different steps required to download, configure, and prepare the Poky Raspberry Pi environment and generate an image that can be used by the target.

## Installing the required packages for the host system

The steps necessary for the configuration of the host system depend on the Linux distribution used. Indeed, it is advisable to use one of the Linux distributions maintained and supported by Poky. This is to avoid wasting time and energy in setting up the host system. Currently, the Yocto Project is supported on the following distributions:

- Ubuntu 12.04 (LTS)
- Ubuntu 13.10
- Ubuntu 14.04 (LTS)
- Fedora release 19 (Schrödinger's Cat)
- Fedora release 21
- CentOS release 6.4
- CentOS release 7.0
- Debian GNU/Linux 7.0 (Wheezy)
- Debian GNU/Linux 7.1 (Wheezy)

- Debian GNU/Linux 7.2 (Wheezy)
- Debian GNU/Linux 7.3 (Wheezy)
- Debian GNU/Linux 7.4 (Wheezy)
- Debian GNU/Linux 7.5 (Wheezy)
- Debian GNU/Linux 7.6 (Wheezy)
- openSUSE 12.2
- openSUSE 12.3
- openSUSE 13.1

Even if your distribution is not listed here, it does not mean that Poky will not work, but the outcome is not guaranteed. Throughout this book, you will be presented with instructions for using Poky with the Ubuntu distribution. If you want more information about the supported Linux distributions, you can visit this link:
`http://www.yoctoproject.org/docs/current/ref-manual/ref-manual.html`.

# Poky on Ubuntu

The following list shows you the packages required for Poky by function, given a supported Ubuntu or Debian Linux distribution:

- Download tools: wget and git-core
- Decompression tools: unzip and tar
- Compilation tools: gcc-multilib, build-essential, and chrpath
- String-manipulation tools: sed and gawk
- Document-management tools: texinfo, xsltproc, docbook-utils, fop, dblatex, and xmlto
- Patch-management tools: patch and diffstat

To summarize, here is the command to type on a headless system:

```
$ sudo apt-get install gawk wget git-core diffstat unzip
texinfo gcc-multilib build-essential chrpath
```

# Poky on Fedora

If you want to use Poky on Fedora, you just have to type this command line:

```
$ sudo yum install gawk make wget tar bzip2 gzip python unzip
perl patch diffutils diffstat git cpp gcc gcc-c++ glibc-devel
texinfo chrpath ccache perl-Data-Dumper perl-Text-ParseWords
perl-Thread-Queue socat
```

# Downloading the Poky metadata

After having installed all the necessary packages, it is time to download the source from Poky. This is done through the Git tool:

```
$ git clone git://git.yoctoproject.org/poky (branch master)
```

Another method involves directly downloading a `tar.bz2` file from this repository:
`https://www.yoctoproject.org/downloads`

To avoid all hazardous and problematicmanipulations, it is strongly recommended to create and switch to a specific local branch:

```
$ cd poky
$ git checkout daisy -b work_branch
```

# Downloading the Raspberry Pi BSP metadata

At this stage, we only have the base of the reference system (Poky) and we have no support for the Broadcom BCM SoC. Basically, the BSP proposed by Poky only offers the following targets:

```
$ ls meta/conf/machine/*.conf
beaglebone.conf
edgerouter.conf
genericx86-64.conf
genericx86.conf
mpc8315e-rdb.conf
```

In addition, there are those provided by **OE-Core**:

```
$ ls meta/conf/machine/*.conf
qemuarm64.conf
qemuarm.conf
qemumips64.conf
qemumips.conf
qemuppc.conf
qemux86-64.conf
qemux86.conf
```

Detailed steps to download the code bundle are mentioned in the Preface of this book. Please have a look.
The code bundle for the book is also hosted on GitHub at `https://github.com/PacktPublishing/Yocto-for-Raspberry-Pi`. We also have other code bundles from our rich catalog of books and videos available at `https://github.com/PacktPublishing/`. Check them out!

In order to generate a compatible system for our target, we will spend more time in this stage and download the specific layer (BSP Layer) to the Raspberry PI:

```
$ git clone git://git.yoctoproject.org/meta-raspberrypi
```

If you want to learn more about `git scm`, you can visit the official website:
`http://git-scm.com/`

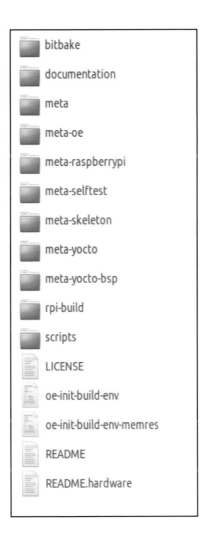

Now, we can verify that we have the configuration**metadata** for our platform (the `rasberrypi.conf` file):

```
$ ls meta-raspberrypi/conf/machine/*.conf
raspberrypi.conf
```

The following screenshot shows the `meta-raspberypi` folder:

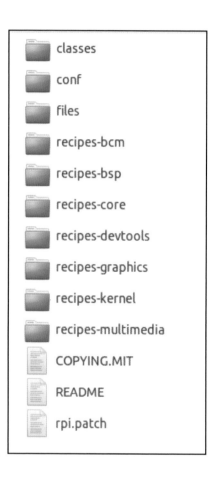

The examples and code presented in this and the following chapters use Yocto Project version 1.7 and Poky version 12.0. For reference, the code name is Dizzy.

Now that we have our environment freshly downloaded, we can proceed with the initialization of our environment and the configuration of our image through various configuration files.

# The oe-init-build-env script

As can be seen in the screenshot before last, the Poky directory contains a script named **oe-init-build-env**. This is a script for the configuration/initialization of the build environment. It is not intended to be executed but must be the **sourced**. Its job, among others, is to initialize a certain number of **environment variables** and place itself in the build directory specified in the argument. The script must be run as follows:

```
$ source oe-init-build-env [build-directory]
```

Here, `build-directory` is an optional parameter for the name of the directory where the environment is set (for example, we can use several build directories in a single Poky source tree). In case it is not specified, it defaults to `build`. The `build-directory` folder is the place where we perform builds. But, in order to standardize the steps, we will use the following command throughout the book to initialize our environment:

```
$ source oe-init-build-env rpi-build
### Shell environment set up for builds. ###
You can now run 'bitbake <target>'
Common targets are:
core-image-minimal
core-image-sato
meta-toolchain
adt-installer
meta-ide-support
You can also run generated qemu images with a command like
'runqemu qemux86'
```

When we initialize a build environment, it creates a directory (the `conf` directory) inside `rpi-build`. This folder contains two important files:

- `local.conf`: This contains parameters to configure Bitbake's behavior.
- `bblayers.conf`: This lists the different layers that Bitbake takes into account in its implementation. The list is assigned to the BBLAYERS variable.

# Editing the local.conf file

The `rpi-build/conf/local.conf` file is a file that can configure every aspect of the build process. It is through this file that we can choose the target machine (the `MACHINE` variable), the distribution (the `DISTRO` variable), the type of package (the `PACKAGE_CLASSES` variable), and the host configuration (`PARALLEL_MAKE`, for example). The minimal set of variables we have to change from the default is the following:

```
BB_NUMBER_THREADS ?= "${@oe.utils.cpu_count()}"
PARALLEL_MAKE ?= "-j ${@oe.utils.cpu_count()}"
MACHINE ?= raspberrypi MACHINE ?= "raspberrypi"
```

The `BB_NUMBER_THREADS` variable determines the number of tasks that BitBake will perform in parallel (these are tasks under Yocto; we're not necessarily talking compilation). By default, in `build/conf/local.conf`, this variable is initialized with `${@oe.utils.cpu_count()}`, corresponding to the number of cores detected on the host system (`/proc/cpuinfo`).

The `PARALLEL_MAKE` variable corresponds to the `-j` to `make` option to specify the number of processes that GNU Make can run in parallel on a compilation task. Again, it is the number of available cores that defines the default value used.

The `MACHINE` variable is where we determine the target machine we wish to build for the Raspberry Pi (defined in the `.conf` file; in our case, it's `raspberrypi.conf`).

# Editing the bblayers.conf file

Now we still have to add the specific layer to our target. This will have the effect of making recipes from this layer available to our build. Therefore, we should edit the `build/conf/bblayers.conf` file:

```
# LAYER_CONF_VERSION is increased each time build/conf
/bblayers.conf
# changes incompatibly
LCONF_VERSION = "6" BBPATH = "${TOPDIR}" BBFILES ?= ""
BBLAYERS ?= " \
/home/packt/RASPBERRYPI/poky/meta \
home/packt/RASPBERRYPI/poky/meta-yocto \
/home/packt/RASPBERRYPI/poky/meta-yocto-bsp \
"BBLAYERS_NON_REMOVABLE ?= " \
/home/packt/RASPBERRYPI/poky/meta \
/home/packt/RASPBERRYPI/poky/meta-yocto \
"
```

Add the following line:

```
# LAYER_CONF_VERSION is increased each time build/conf
/bblayers.conf
# changes incompatibly
LCONF_VERSION = "6" BBPATH = "${TOPDIR}" BBFILES ?= ""
BBLAYERS ?= " \
/home/packt/RASPBERRYPI/poky/meta \
/home/packt/RASPBERRYPI/poky/meta-yocto \
/home/packt/RASPBERRYPI/poky/meta-yocto-bsp \
/home/packt/RASPBERRYPI/poky/meta-raspberrypi \
"BBLAYERS_NON_REMOVABLE ?= " \
/home/packt/RASPBERRYPI/poky/meta \
/home/packt/RASPBERRYPI/poky/meta-yocto \
    "
```

Naturally, you have to adapt the absolute path (`/home/packt/RASPBERRYPI` here) depending on your own installation.

# Building the Poky image

At this stage of development, let's have a look at the available images and certified compatible for our platform (`.bb` files).

## Choice of image

Poky provides several pre-designed image recipes that we can use to build our own binary image. We can check the list of available images by running the following command from the `poky` directory:

```
$ ls meta*/recipes*/images/*.bb
```

All the recipes provide images that are, in essence, sets of unpacked and configured packages, generating a filesystem that we can use on actual hardware (for further information about different images, you can visit (`http://www.yoctoproject.org/docs/latest/mega-manual/mega-manual.html#ref-images`).

Next, here's a brief representation of available images:

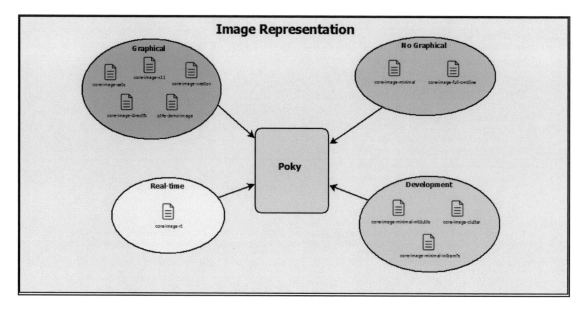

We can add the layers proposed by **meta-raspberry** to all of these layers:

```
$ ls meta-raspberrypi/recipes-core/images/*.bb
rpi-basic-image.bb
rpi-hwup-image.bb
rpi-test-image.bb
```

- `rpi-hwup-image.bb`: This is an image based on core-image-minimal.
- `rpi-basic-image.bb`: This is an image based on `rpi-hwup-image.bb` with some added features (a splash screen).
- `rpi-test-image.bb`: This is an image based on `rpi-basic-image.bb` and includes some packages present in `meta-raspberrypi`.

We will choose one of these three recipes for the rest of this chapter. Note that these files (`.bb`) describe recipes, like all the others. These are organized logically, and here, we have the ones for creating an image for the Raspberry Pi.

# Running BitBake

At this point, we need to start **BitBake**, the build engine, which will parse all the recipes that contain the image you pass as a parameter (for our first example, we can take `rpi-basic-image`):

```
$ bitbake rpi-basic-image
Loading cache: 100%
|#################################################################
#################################################################
##################| ETA:  00:00:00
Loaded 1352 entries from dependency cache.
NOTE: Resolving any missing task queue dependencies
Build Configuration:
BB_VERSION = "1.25.0"
BUILD_SYS = "x86_64-linux"
NATIVELSBSTRING = "Ubuntu-14.04"
TARGET_SYS = "arm-poky-linux-gnueabi"
MACHINE = "raspberrypi"
DISTRO = "poky"
DISTRO_VERSION = "1.7"
TUNE_FEATURES = "arm armv6 vfp"
TARGET_FPU = "vfp"
meta
meta-yocto
meta-yocto-bsp =
"master:08d3f44d784e06f461b7d83ae9262566f1cf09e4"
meta-raspberrypi =
"master:6c6f44136f7e1c97bc45be118a48bd9b1fef1072"
NOTE: Preparing RunQueue
NOTE: Executing SetScene Tasks
NOTE: Executing RunQueue Tasks
```

Once launched, Bitbake begins by browsing all the files (`.bb`, `.bbclass`) that the environment provides access to and storing the information in a cache.

While the parser of Bitbake is parallelized, the first execution will always be longer (only by about a few seconds) because it has to build the cache. However, subsequent executions will be almost instantaneous because Bitbake load the cache. As we can see from the previous command, before executing the task list, Bitbake displays a trace that details the versions used (target, version, OS, and so on). And finally, Bitbake starts the execution of the tasks and displays the progress.

Depending on your setup, you can go drink some coffee or even eat some pizza. Usually, after this, if all goes well, you will be pleased to find that the `tmp/` sub directory's directory construction (`rpi-build`) is generally populated. The build directory (`rpi-build`) contains about 20 GB after the creation of the image.

After a few hours of baking, we can rejoice with the result and the creation of the system image for our target:

```
$ ls rpi-build/tmp/deploy/images/raspberrypi/*sdimg
rpi-basic-image-raspberrypi.rpi-sdimg
```

It is this file that will serve us to create our bootable SD card.

# Creating an SD card

Now that your environment is complete, you can create an SD card with the following command (*remember to change /dev/sdX to the proper device name and be careful not to kill your hard disk by selecting the wrong device name*):

```
$ sudo dd if=rpi-basic-image-raspberrypi.rpi-sdimg of=/dev/sdX
bs=1M
```

Once the copying is complete, you can check whether the operation was successful using the following command (see `mmcblk0`):

```
$ lsblk
NAME            MAJ:MIN RM    SIZE RO TYPE MOUNTPOINT
mmcblk0          179:0    0   3,7G  0 disk
â??â??mmcblk0p1 179:1    0    20M  0 part
/media/packt/raspberrypi
â??â??mmcblk0p2 179:2    0   108M  0 part /media/packt/f075d6df-d8b8-4e85-
a2e4-36f3d4035c3c
```

You could also look at the left-hand side of your interface:

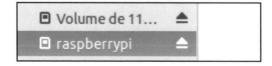

# Booting the image on the Raspberry Pi

We now come to what is surely the most anticipated moment of this chapter: the moment where we boot our Raspberry Pi with a fresh Poky image.

You just have to insert your SD card into a slot, connect the HDMI cable to your monitor, and connect the power supply (it is also recommended to used a mouse and keyboard to shut down the device, unless you plan on just pulling the power and possibly corrupting the boot partition).

After connecting the power supply, you should see the Raspberry Pi splash screen:

 The login for the Yocto/Poky distribution is `root`.

# Summary

In this chapter, we learned the steps required to set up Poky and get our first image built. We ran that image on the Raspberry Pi, which gave us a good overview of the available capabilities.

In the next chapter, you will be introduced to Hob, which provides a human-friendly interface for Bitbake. We will use it to build an image and customize it further. After that, you will be introduced to another tool, Toaster, which is a web interface for Bitbake.

# 3
# Mastering Baking with Hob and Toaster

In this chapter, we will explore two powerful tools included in the Yocto Project. In the first part of the chapter, we will speak about Hob, which is a graphical interface for BitBake. In the second part, we will work with Toaster, a web interface that enables you to follow the advanced parts of the build with a simple browser (such as Firefox).

## Hob

In order to explore Hob, we will, through this section, sweep through the different essential steps for its proper functioning.

## Preparing the environment for Hob

As in Chapter 2, *Building our First Poky Image for the Raspberry Pi,* the first step is to initialize the environment. Recall this command:

```
$ source oe-init-build-env rpi-build
```

Once the command is launched, the terminal will be redirected to the rpi-build directory.

# Running Hob

Now that we have initialized all the variables required to build, we can start the Hob interface with this command:

```
$ hob
```

Once you run this command, Hob will try to parse the configuration files (`local.conf` and `bblayers.conf`) in order to find the metadata available to create the image. After this step, you will see the interface launch screen, as shown here:

Now, we can choose the desired machine from the list offered by Hob. Select the **raspberrypi** machine.

 The machine option you choose corresponds to the MACHINE variable in the local.conf file.

You will see the following progress screen:

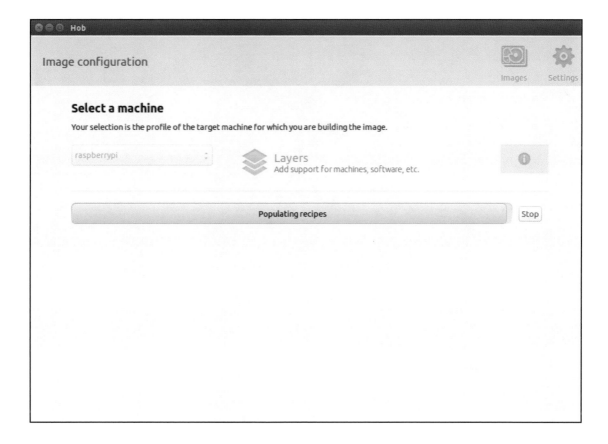

Adding a layer is very simple. We just have to click on the **Layers** button, as shown in this screenshot:

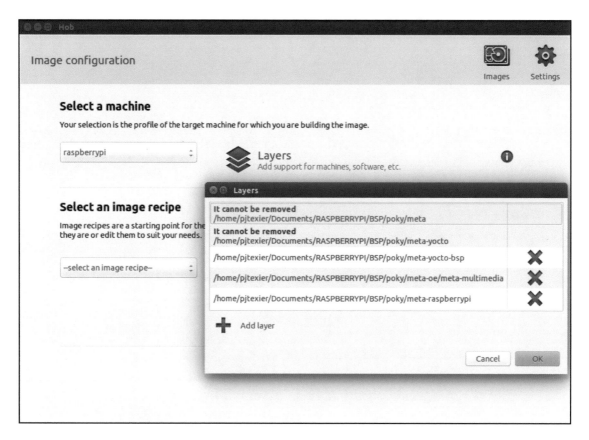

After choosing the target machine, we need to choose he image that we want to create.

Like in Chapter 2, *Building our First Poky Image for the Raspberry Pi*, we will select **rpi-basic-image** for our example:

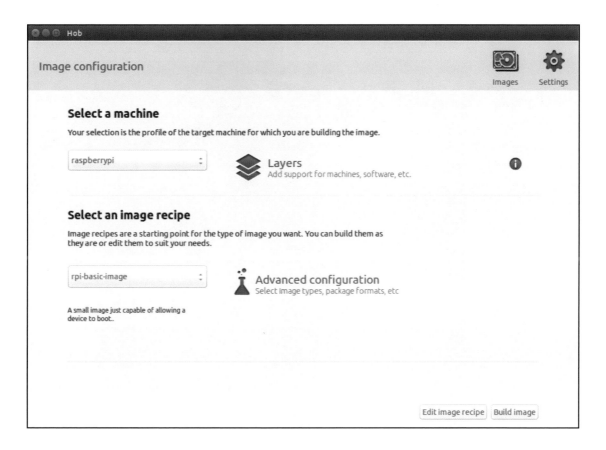

The next step (*if you want to modify the default configuration*) is to select advanced configuration options by clicking on **Advanced configuration**, as shown in the following two screenshots. These options could be image types (such as `cpio.gz`, `ext2.bz2`, and `ext3.gz`) or package formats (IPK, DEB, or RPM).

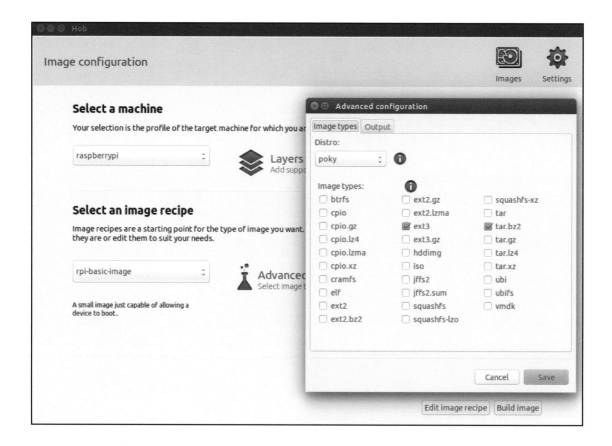

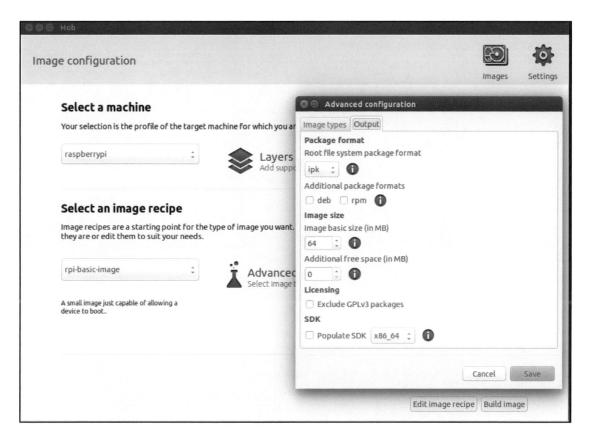

At this point, we can build the final image by clicking on the **Build Image** button. If you want to modify the recipe of an image, you just have to click on the **Edit Image Recipe** button.

# Configuring recipes and packages

You can see the list of included recipes in Hob in the following screenshot:

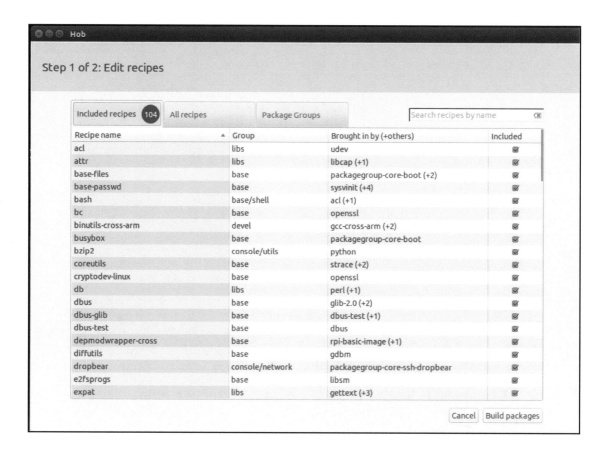

As you can see, it is easy to add or remove recipes for the configuration of our image by selecting or deselecting them. If you click on the recipe name, you can see details such as its version and license. The next step is to click on the **Build packages** button. Once you do this, you will see the following screen:

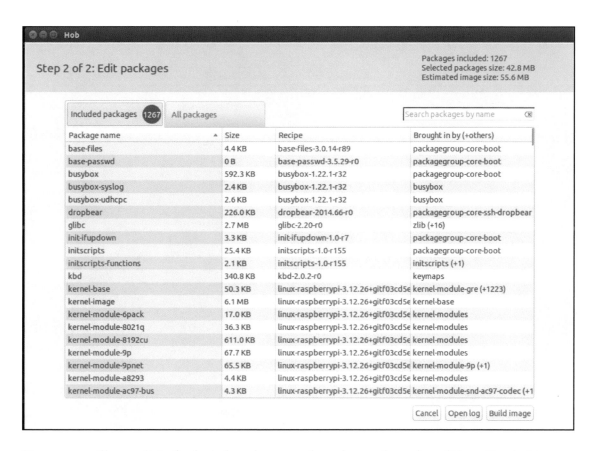

Here, you will see a list of selected packages and can know the value of the estimated image size (in the top-right corner) and decide to remove some applications in order to generate a smaller image. It is also possible to see the number of selected packages and the size of the selected packages.

BitBake resolves all dependencies from the selected packages, including any required additional packages.

# Building the image

As you can imagine, the last step consists of building our image (by clicking on **Build image**). Hob tracks the progress of the construction, as shown in this screenshot:

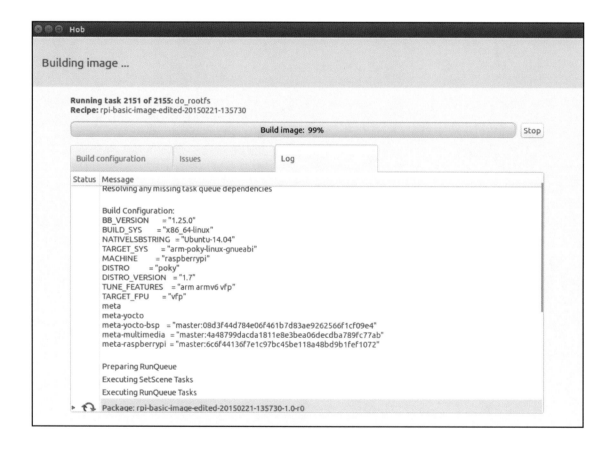

You will see this screen when the build has completed:

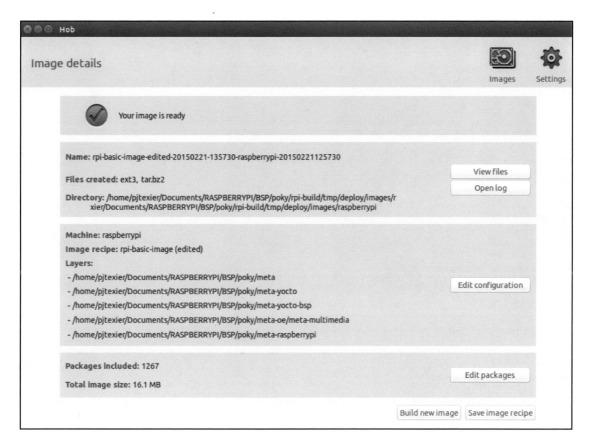

On this screen, Hob displays a summary of the build. It is possible to go to the directory where the files have been generated (`rpi- build/tmp/deploy/images/raspberrypi/`), and you can also view the log of the build process.

After that, we can create a bootable SD card with our Hob Image for the Raspberry Pi:

```
$ sudo dd if=rpi-basic-image-edited-20150221-135730-raspberrypi.rpi- sdimg
of=/dev/sdX bs=1M
```

At this point, we just have to put the SD card into the Raspberry Pi, turn on the board, and play with it.

# Exploring Toaster

Toaster is a web interface for BitBake. The Yocto Project website describes it as follows:

*"Toaster is an Application Programming Interface (API) and web-based interface to the OpenEmbedded build system, which uses BitBake. Currently, Toaster collects and presents information about your builds, which you can navigate and query using a web browser"*

# Installing the required packages for the host system

In order to use Toaster correctly on your preferred Linux distribution, you need to install Django and South:

```
$ sudo pip install django==1.6
$ sudo pip install South==0.8.4
```

> The `pip` command makes it easy to install Python modules, in the same way you install packages in a Linux distribution.

# Running Toaster

Now that our system is ready to use Toaster, we only have to run it using the following command in order to launch the service:

```
$ source toaster start
```

This will give you the following output:

```
The system will start. Syncing... Creating tables ... Installing custom SQL
... Installing indexes ... Installed 0 object(s) from 0 fixture(s) Synced:
> django.contrib.staticfiles  > django.contrib.humanize  > south Not synced
(use migrations):  - orm  - bldcontrol (use ./manage.py migrate to migrate
these) Running migrations for orm: - Nothing to migrate.  - Loading initial
data for orm. Installed 0 object(s) from 0 fixture(s) Starting webserver
Webserver address:  http://0.0.0.0:8000/ Bitbake server address: 0.0.0.0,
server port: 54693 Successful start.
```

We now have our web interface available at http://0.0.0.0:8000/.

# Running BitBake

At the moment, Toaster doesn't support configuration through the interface (Future releases of Toaster will add build-running and build-customization capabilities). Toaster collects and presents information about your builds, which you can navigate and query using a web browser. So, we have to manually start BitBake to monitor the progress of build. As in Chapter 2, *Building our First Poky Image for the Raspberry Pi* , we can launch the build process using the following command:

```
$ bitbake rpi-basic-image
```

The build process will progress as follows:

```
Loading cache: 100%
|###########################################################################
###########################################################################
##################| ETA:  00:00:00 Loaded 1352 entries from dependency
cache. NOTE: Resolving any missing task queue dependencies Build
Configuration: BB_VERSION        = "1.25.0" BUILD_SYS          = "x86_64-
linux" NATIVELSBSTRING   = "Ubuntu-14.04" TARGET_SYS        = "arm-poky-
linux-gnueabi" MACHINE        = "raspberrypi" DISTRO            = "poky"
DISTRO_VERSION    = "1.7" TUNE_FEATURES      = "arm armv6 vfp" TARGET_FPU
= "vfp" meta            meta-yocto        meta-yocto-bsp      =
"master:08d3f44d784e06f461b7d83ae9262566f1cf09e4" meta-raspberrypi    =
"master:6c6f44136f7e1c97bc45be118a48bd9b1fef1072" NOTE: Preparing RunQueue
NOTE: Executing SetScene Tasks NOTE: Executing RunQueue Tasks
```

# Running the web interface

Now that we have launched BitBake, we can monitor the progress of the process (the build process), as shown in the following screenshot. Note that the best way to open the Toaster interface is to navigate to it (using hyperlinks).

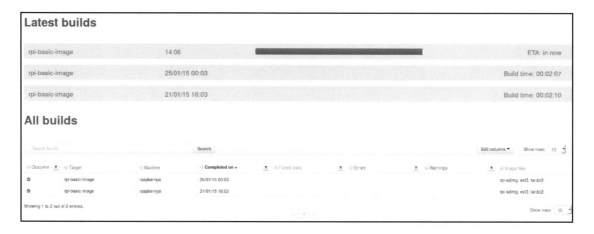

Toaster is still in the development phase; it is likely to become a worthy replacement of Hob. Indeed, the development team wants to make BitBake fully configurable via the web interface.

# Summary

In this chapter, we discovered how to use user-friendly interfaces such as Hob and Toaster. We learned the different capabilities of these tools (configuration and functionality). It is worth noting that these tools allow better flexibility for development teams.

In the next chapter, we will learn the main role played by BitBake within the Yocto Project. We will discover the different tasks that enable us to generate packages for our image.

# 4

# Understanding BitBake

In this chapter, we will initially explore the metadata (the basic concept) and recipes that are used by Poky (the dependencies among them). We will then look at the different ways in which BitBake downloads source code. We will end this chapter by presenting the tasks used by BitBake to get to the creation of the root filesystem image.

## BitBake

As presented in Chapter 1, *Meeting the Yocto Project*, **BitBake** is a task scheduler (like GNU Make) that parses shell and Python scripts. The code parsed generates and runs tasks (configure, compile, and so on), which are basically sets of steps ordered according to the code's dependencies.

Here are some points taken directly from the BitBake user manual:

- BitBake executes tasks according to the provided metadata, which builds up the tasks. Metadata is stored in recipe (`.bb`), configuration (`.conf`), and class (`.bbclass`) files and provides BitBake with instructions on what tasks to run and the dependencies between those tasks.
- BitBake includes a fetcher library for obtaining source code from various places, such as source control systems or websites.

- The instructions for each unit to be built (such as a piece of software) are known as recipe files and contain all the information about the unit (dependencies, source file locations, checksums, description, and so on).
- BitBake includes a client/server abstraction, can be used from a command line or as a service over XMLRPC, and has several different user interfaces.

# Metadata

The metadata used by BitBake can be in several distinct forms; they are as follows:

- Configuration (`.conf`) files
- Recipes (`.bb` and `.bbappend` files)
- Classes (`.bbclass` files)
- Include (`.inc`) files

# Configuration

**Configuration files**, which are denoted by the `.conf` extension, define various configuration variables that govern the project's build process. These files fall into several areas that define machine configuration options, distribution configuration options, compiler tuning options, general common configuration options, and user configuration options.

# Classes

**Class files**, which are denoted by the `.bbclass` extension, contain information that is useful to share between metadata files. The BitBake source tree currently comes with one class metadata file called `base.bbclass`. You can find this file in the `classes` directory. The `base.bbclass` file is special since it is always included automatically for all recipes and classes. This class contains definitions for standard basic tasks such as fetching, unpacking, configuring (empty by default), compiling (runs any makefile present), installing (empty by default), and packaging (empty by default). These tasks are often overridden or extended by other classes added during the project development process.

# Recipes

BitBake **recipes**, which are denoted by the `.bb` file extension (for example, `bcm2835_1.38.bb`), are the most basic metadata files. These recipe files provide BitBake with the following information:

- Descriptive information about the package
- The version of the recipe
- Existing dependencies
- Where the source code resides
- Whether the source code requires any patches
- How to compile the source code
- Where on the target machine to install the package being compiled

# Parsing metadata

The first thing BitBake does is parse base configuration metadata (`.conf` files). Base configuration metadata consists of the `bblayers.conf` file to determine what layers BitBake needs to recognize, all necessary `layer.conf` files (one from each layer), and `bitbake.conf`. The data itself is of various types:

- Recipes: These contain details about particular pieces of software.
- Class data: This provides an abstraction of common build information (for example, how to build a Linux kernel).
- Configuration data: This provides machine-specific settings, policy decisions, and so forth. Configuration data acts as the glue that binds everything together.

The `layer.conf` files are used to construct key variables such as `BBPATH` and `BBFILES`. `BBPATH` is used to search for configuration and class files under the `conf/` and `class/` directories, respectively. `BBFILES` is used to find recipe files (`.bb` and `.bbappend`). If there is no `bblayers.conf` file, it is assumed that the user has set the `BBPATH` and `BBFILES` variables directly in the environment.

Next, the `bitbake.conf` file is searched using the `BBPATH` variable that was just constructed. The `bitbake.conf` file may also include other configuration files using the `include` or `require` directives.

# Preferences and providers

Once BitBake has realized the "parsing" step (analyzing all the recipes), it must know how to build the target. It starts by looking through the `PROVIDES` variable set in the recipe files. The default `PROVIDES` value for a recipe is its name (`PN`).

PN represents the name of the recipe; PR, the revision of the recipe; and PV, the version of the recipe. For example, when using the recipe `rpio-gpio_0.5.9.bb`, here is what the values will be:

`${PN} = rpi-gpio`

`${PV} = 0.5.9`

Sometimes, a target might have multiple providers. A common example is *virtual/kernel*, which is provided by each kernel recipe (check out `meta-raspberrypi/tree/master/recipes-kernel/linux` for further information). Each machine often selects the best kernel provider by using a line similar to the following in the machine configuration file. If we look into this following file (`meta-raspberrypi/conf/machine/include/rpi-default-providers.inc`), we can see some variables:

```
# RaspberryPi BSP default providers
PREFERRED_PROVIDER_virtual/kernel = ""linux-raspberrypi""
PREFERRED_PROVIDER_u-boot = ""u-boot-rpi""
```

In this case, we have selected the required U-Boot version and kernel for our Raspberry Pi.

# Dependencies

In order to satisfy dependencies, the recipes must declare what they need to have available during the build process.

BitBake use a special mechanism that allows us to list the build-time dependencies and then checks whether all of the rules are satisfied before the build step. For example, if you work with canutils (`http://pengutronix.de/software/socket-can/download/canutils/`), you have to set this following variable:

```
DEPENDS = "libsocketcan"
```

In this example, **CANUTILS** needs *libsocketcan*; therefore, BitBake will start by building the `libsocketcan` package (and installing the headers into rootfs) before building canutils and linking.

When an application depends on something to run, it is called a runtime dependency (these are packages necessary on the target in order to guarantee proper functioning). In this case, we don't need to set the `DEPENDS` variable but the `RDEPENDS` variable in a recipe in order to inform BitBake.

# Fetching

The mechanism used by BitBake to fetch source code is internally called the **fetcher backend**. There are several fetcher backends supported, which can be configured to align user requirements and optimize source code fetching.

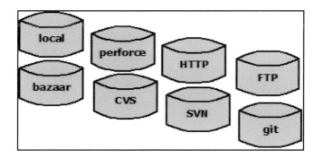

BitBake supports several protocols for remote file downloads. The most commonly used are `http://`, `https://`, and `git://`. When BitBake executes the `do_fetch` task in a recipe, it checks the contents of `SRC_URI`. We will discover, through the various fetchers, how to proceed based on our need.

# The local file fetcher

The local file fetcher submodule handles URLs that begin with `file://`. The filename you specify within the URL can either be an absolute or relative path to a file. For example, with a file called `my_source_file.c`, we must write the `SRC_URI` attribute's content like this:

```
SRC_URI = "file://my_source_file.c"
```

# The HTTP fetcher

The HTTP fetcher obtains files from web servers. Internally, the fetcher uses the wget utility.

In this example, we will use the `bcm2835` library. With this submodule, we will retrieve the `tar.gz` file of this library:

```
SRC_URI = "http://www.open.com.au/mikem/bcm2835/bcm2835-${PV}.tar.gz"
```

# The Git fetcher

One of the most commonly used source control management systems in use is Git. BitBake has solid support for it, and the Git backend is used when the `do_fetch` task is run and finds a `git://` URL at the `SRC_URI` variable. Here is an example featuring a utility developed by Christophe Blaess. It is a simple command-line tool to help with the use of Linux spidev devices.

```
SRCREV = "cc6a41fdcec60610703ba6db488c621c64952898"
```

This variable contains the reference to the *commit* that the version control system will use as a basis. In the case of Git, it is the the commit hash.

```
SRC_URI = "git://github.com/cpb-/spi-tools.git;protocol=git"
```

 When the `SRCREV` variable points to a hash not available in the master branch, we need to use the `branch=<branch name>` parameter, as follows: `SRC_URI = git://myserver/myrepo.git;branch=mybranch`. In the cases when the hash used points to a tag that is not available in a branch, we need to use the `nobranch=1` option, as follows: `SRC_URI = "git://myserver/myrepo.git;nobranch=1"`.

For further information about the `SRC_URI` parameter's values, go to `http://www.yoctoproject.org/docs/1.6/bitbake-user-manual/bitbake-user-manual.html#var-SRC_URI` for some examples.

# Understanding BitBake's tasks

The `bitbake` command is the primary interface to the BitBake tool. This chapter presents the `bitbake` command syntax and provides several execution examples.

For example, if you want to build a specific recipe, run the following command:

```
$ bitbake <recipe>
```

BitBake runs a set of scheduled tasks. When we wish to run a specific task, we can use the following command:

```
$ bitbake <recipe> -c <task>
```

If you want to clean a specific package (`spitools`, for example), you just have to run this:

```
$ bitbake spitools -c clean
```

To list the tasks defined for a recipe, we can use the following command:

```
$ bitbake <recipe> -c listtasks
```

Here is a description of BitBake tasks:

- **do_fetch**: The first step when building a recipe is fetching the required source. This is done using the fetching backend feature we discussed previously. It is important to point out that fetching source or a file does not mean it is a remote source. In fact, every file required during the recipe build must be fetched so that it is made available in the `WORKDIR` directory.

  All downloaded content is stored in the download folder (the `DL_DIR` variable), so all external source code is cached to avoid redownloading it every time we need the same source.

- **do_unpack**: The natural subsequent task after the `do_fetch` task is `do_unpack`. It is responsible for unpacking source code or checking the requested revision or branch in case the referenced source uses an SCM system.

- **do_patch**: Once the source code has been properly unpacked, BitBake initiates the process of adapting it. This is done by the `do_patch` task. Every file fetched by `do_fetch` that has the `.patch` extension is assumed to be a patch to be applied. This task applies the list of required patches.

   > The process of applying a patch uses the `S` variable, which points to the source code. The default value used for `S` is ${WORKDIR}/${PN}-${PV}, and it is used for the `do_patch`, `do_configure`, `do_compile`, and `do_install` tasks.

- **do_configure**, **do_compile**, and **do_install**: The `do_configure`, `do_compile`, and `do_install` tasks are performed in this order. Some recipes may omit one task or another. It is important to note that the environment variables defined in the tasks are different from one task to another.

   > Tasks vary a lot from one recipe to another. Poky provides a rich collection of predefined tasks in the classes, which ought to be used when possible. For example, when the `Autotools` class is inherited by a recipe, it provides a known implementation for the `do_configure`, `do_compile`, and `do_install` tasks.

- **do_package**: The `do_package` task splits the files installed by the recipe into logical components, such as debugging symbols, documentation, and libraries. The `do_package` task ensures that files are split up and packaged correctly.

One of the most common uses of Poky is the generation of the root filesystem. The `rootfs` image should be seen as a ready-to-use root filesystem for a target. The `rootfs` is basically a directory with the desired packages installed. The list of packages to be installed into `rootfs` is defined by a union of packages listed by `IMAGE_INSTALL` and the packages included by `IMAGE_FEATURES`.

 After `do_rootfs` has finished, the generated image file is placed in `<build-dir>/tmp/deploy/image/raspberrypi/`.

We will learn more about the process and its contents in `Chapter 5`, *Creating, Developing, and Deploying on the Raspberry Pi*.

# Summary

In this chapter, we discovered most of BitBake's functionalities. We also learned how BitBake works in order for us to generate some packages for our Raspberry Pi.

In the next chapter, we will learn how to develop within the Yocto Project. We will write recipes, create SDKs, and more.

# 5

# Creating, Developing, and Deploying on the Raspberry Pi

In this chapter, we will cover the basic concept of Yocto/OE in order to integrate a custom application with the Raspberry Pi. We will learn how to generate an SDK for a cross-compiling application. We'll also discuss package management.

After that, we will create our own application and recipe in order to deploy it on the Raspberry Pi through the Yocto Project.

## Software development kits (SDKs)

An SDK is a set of tools we can use outside **Yocto/OE**. These tools generally include a compiler, linker, debugger, libraries, and external headers. This set of compilation tools is called a **toolchain**. With the Raspberry Pi (or other embedded platforms), the toolchain is often composed of crosstools, which are tools executed on one architecture that produce a binary for use in another architecture.

The following figure depicts the process of cross-compilation:

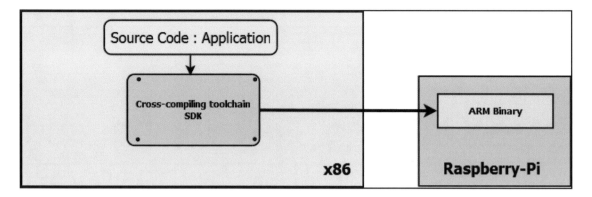

The **Yocto/OE** build system can be used to generate a cross-compilation toolchain and matching sysroot folder for a target system.

The sysroot folder contains the shared libraries, headers, and utilities that are used in the process of building recipes,

With this build system, there are several ways of generating an SDK that conforms to our Raspberry Pi platform.

# A generic SDK – meta-toolchain

The meta-toolchainrecipe will build a toolchain that matches the Raspberry Pi platform and a basic sysroot (generic SDK) that does not match our target root filesystem. However, this toolchain can be used to build software such as the U-Boot bootloader, the Linux kernel, or simple applications that do not need a `sysroot` folder. We can generate this toolchain with the following command:

```
$ source oe-init-build-env rpi-build
$ bitbake meta-toolchain
```

Once it has been built, we can install it like this:

```
$ cd poky/rpi-build/tmp/deploy/sdk
$ ./poky-eglibc-x86_64-meta-toolchain-qt5-armv6-vfp-toolchain- 1.7.1.sh
```

# image.bb -c populate_sdk

The populate task is the best and recommended way of building a toolchain matching the Raspberry Pi platform with a `sysroot` folder matching our target root filesystem. We can generate this toolchain with the following command:

```
$ bitbake rpi-basic-image.bb -c populate_sdk
```

We can install it with these commands:

```
$ cd tmp/deploy/sdk
$ ./poky-eglibc-x86_64-meta-toolchain-qt-armv6-vfp-toolchain-1.7.1.sh
```

The following figure is a summary of the populate task, taken directly from the Yocto Project Manual (`http://www.yoctoproject.org/docs/current/ref-manual/ref-manual.html#sdk-dev-environment`):

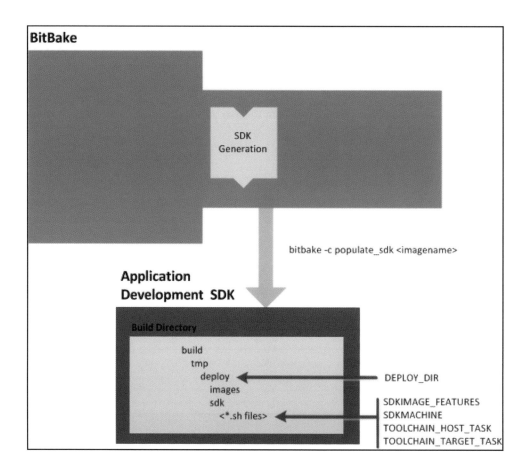

# The Qt SDK – meta-toolchain-qt

The `meta-toolchain-qt` toolchain is just an extension of `meta-toolchain` and includes support for compiling Qt applications (graphical or non-graphical). We can generate this toolchain with the following command:

```
$ bitbake meta-toolchain-qt
```

Once it has been built, we can install it with these commands:

```
$ cd tmp/deploy/sdk
$ ./poky-eglibc-x86_64-meta-toolchain-qt-armv6-vfp-toolchain-1.7.1.sh
```

# The Qt5 SDK – meta-toolchain-qt5

This toolchain is just an extension of `meta-toolchain-qt`, including support for compiling Qt5 applications. We can generate it with the following command:

```
$ bitbake meta-toolchain-qt5
```

Once it has been built, we can install it with these commands:

```
$ cd tmp/deploy/sdk
$ ./poky-eglibc-x86_64-meta-toolchain-qt5-armv6-vfp-toolchain- 1.7.1.sh
```

The SDK can be designed for use on a 32-bit or 64-bit Linux distribution, and that depends on the host architecture in which the SDK is generated. The selection is made by setting the `SDKMACHINE` variable (in `conf/local.conf`), which can take `i686` or `x86_64` as values, like this, for example:

```
SDKMACHINE? = "X86_64"
```

# Cross-compilation – an example

In order to validate the proper functioning of our toolchain, we can try to compile an application.

## Configuration of the SDK environment

The first thing to do is source the environment variable for our toolchain. Use either of these commands:

```
$ source /opt/poky/1.7.1/environment-setup-armv6-vfp poky-linux-
gnueabi
$ . ./opt/poky/1.7.1/environment-setup-armv6-vfp poky-linux-gnueabi
```

# List of tools

After this, our toolchain is in our system `PATH` variable, and we can take a look at all of the tools in the toolchain:

```
$ arm-poky-linux-gnueabi-arm-poky-linux-gnueabi-addr2line arm-poky-linux-
gnueabi-elfedit arm-poky-linux-gnueabi-gcc-ranlib arm-poky-linux-gnueabi-
ld.bfd arm-poky-linux-gnueabi-readelf
arm-poky-linux-gnueabi-ar arm-poky-linux-gnueabi-g++ arm-poky-linux-
gnueabi-gcov arm-poky-linux-gnueabi-nm arm-poky-linux-gnueabi-size
arm-poky-linux-gnueabi-as arm-poky-linux-gnueabi-gcc arm-poky-linux-
gnueabi-gdb arm-poky-linux-gnueabi-objcopy arm-poky-linux-gnueabi-strings
arm-poky-linux-gnueabi-c++filt arm-poky-linux-gnueabi-gcc-ar arm-poky-
linux-gnueabi-gprof arm-poky-linux-gnueabi-objdump arm-poky-linux-gnueabi-
strip
arm-poky-linux-gnueabi-cpp arm-poky-linux-gnueabi-gcc-nm arm-poky-linux-
gnueabi-ld arm-poky-linux-gnueabi-ranlib
```

We can find our compiler (`arm-poky-linux-gnueabi-gcc` or `arm-poky-linux-gnueabi-g++` for C++ applications), our debugger (`arm-poky-linux-gnueabi-gdb`), some binary tools (GNU Binary Utilities), and so on.

# Compilation

Now, we can compile our first application with the external toolchain:

```
$ ${CC} -o hello_world_packt hello_world_packt.c
$ file hello_world_packthello_world_packt: ELF 32-bit LSB executable,  ARM,
EABI5 version 1 (SYSV), dynamically linked (uses shared libs),  for
GNU/Linux 2.6.32,  BuildID[sha1]=1c2b89895d89b1868884295756214d609748f2c2,
not stripped
```

# Raspberry Pi and a package manager

The basic building block of the Yocto Project is the generation of packages; therefore, it is possible to include a package manager to our Yocto distribution (similar to a Linux distribution, for example). Indeed, after the generation of the image (refer Chapter 2), it contains no package manager, so this means that our image is not updateable (similar to a firmware, for example).

The inclusion of a package manager in our distribution is done through this variable, if adding it to `conf/local.conf`:

```
EXTRA_IMAGE_FEATURES += "package-management"
```

If adding to a recipe file (such as `rpi-basic-image.bb`), use this instead:

```
IMAGE_FEATURES += "package-management"
```

With this addition, we have now an image with a package manager that is more flexible, updateable, and more industrial. Here's how to install a package with the `opkg` package manager:

```
$ opkg install package_name.ipk
```

# Package format availablility

Bitbake (the task scheduler) supports the following package formats:

RPM: Originally used by Red Hat due to its name, Red Hat Package Manager, it is now used by other distributions (openSUSE, for example).

DEB: The Debian package format is used by Debian and derivate distributions such as Ubuntu.

IPK: This stands for Itsy Package Management System (originally of the handhelds.org project). It is a lightweight package management system designed for embedded systems (such as the Gumstix platform: `http://gumstix.org/add-software-packages.html`). OpenEmbedded-Core, and as a consequence Poky, uses the `opkg` package manager to support the IPK format.

> If you are an Android enthusiast, you can make an analogy with the **APK** package format.

# Choosing a package format

Support for the formats is provided using a set of classes (`package_rpm`, `package_deb`, and `package_ipk`). The choice of the package formats depends very much on project needs. Factors to consider include the following:

- Memory footprint
- Resource usage,
- Speed of installation

> By default, Poky uses the **RPM** (Red Hat Package Manager) package format.

The selection of package format is done through the `PACKAGE_CLASSES` variable in the `conf/local.conf` file.

Type this to include the RPM package format:

```
PACKAGE_CLASSES ?= "package_rpm"
```

Type this to include the DEB package format:

```
PACKAGE_CLASSES ?= "package_deb"
```

Type this to include the IPK package format:

```
PACKAGE_CLASSES ?= "package_ipk"
```

 It is possible to specify several package formats but, to build images, Bitbake searches based on the first package format in the PACKAGE_CLASSES variable: PACKAGE_CLASSES ?= "package_rpm package_deb package_ipk"

# Installing and updating a package on the target

Now that we have coveredpackage formats, we will see how to integrate them with the Raspberry Pi.

# RPM packages

With RPM packages, it is possible to use (after copying it to the target) RPM or SMART utilities to install packages on the Raspberry Pi.

## Installing manually

To manually install RPM packages, use one of these commands:

```
$ rpm -ivh package_name.rpm
$ smart install package_name.rpm
```

## Installing automatically

During the development and debugging phases, it may be worthwhile for the developer to update the packages (binaries) on the target (Raspberry Pi) without having to handle many Linux commands.

The first step consists of creating the package index in our repository (in order to use package feeds):

```
$ source oe-init-build-env rpi-build
$ bitbake package-index
```

After that, we can install a web server (such as `lighttpd`):

```
$ sudo apt-get install lighttpd
```

By default, the document root specified in the `/etc/lighttpd/lighttpd.conf` configuration file is `/var/www/`:

```
$ tree /var/www/
/var/www/
html
amod.png
formulaire.html
index.html
logo.png
play_48.png
index.lighttpd.html
1 directory, 6 files
```

So, we only need a symlink to our package feed:

```
$ mkdir /var/www/rpi-deploy
$ ln -s rpi-build/tmp/deploy/rpm /var/www/rpi-deploy/rpm
```

At this point, you need to restart the `lighttpd` server:

```
$ sudo /etc/init.d/lighttpd restart
```

On the Raspberry Pi, we need to inform `smart` of every package database we want to use. For example, for the `all` directory in `rpi-deploy/rpm`, we will need to issue this command:

```
$ smart channel --add all type=rpm-md baseurl=http://<server-ip> /rpi-deploy/rpm/all
```

Now that our environment is in place, we can query and update packages from the Raspberry Pi's root filesystem with the following commands:

```
$ smart update
$ smart query <package_name>
$ smart install <package_name>
$ smart query -installed
```

Here's an example of removing a package from the Raspberry Pi (the Monkey web server):

```
$ smart remove monkey
Updating cache..
############################################################################
######################### [100%]
Computing transaction...
Removing packages (1):
monkey-1.5.4-r0@armv6-vfp
479.4kB will be freed. Confirm changes? (Y/n): Y
Committing transaction...
Preparing...##############################################################
################################### [  0%]
Stopping Monkey HTTP Server: stopped /usr/bin/monkey (pid 1448)
monkey
Output from monkey:(  0%)
warning: /etc/monkey/sites/default saved as
/etc/monkey/sites/default.rpmsave
warning: /etc/monkey/plugins/logger/logger.conf saved as
/etc/monkey/plugins/logger/logger.conf.rpmsave
warning: /etc/monkey/plugins.load saved as /etc/monkey/plugins.load.rpmsave
1:Removing monkey
############################################################################
######################### [100%]
Removing any system startup links for monkey ...
/etc/rc0.d/K70monkey /etc/rc1.d/K70monkey /etc/rc2.d/S70monkey
/etc/rc3.d/S70monkey /etc/rc4.d/S70monkey /etc/rc5.d/S70monkey
/etc/rc6.d/K70monkey Saving cache...
```

More information and a user manual for the smart utility can be found at https://labix.org/smart/.

# IPK packages

With IPK packages, it is possible to use (after copy the package to the target) OPKG utilities to install the package on the Raspberry Pi.

## Installing manually

To manually install an IPK package, use this command:

```
$ opkg install package_name.ipk
```

## Installing automatically

For the management of IPK packages, it is easy to create a package repository on our development workstation.

The first step is to add to `conf/local.conf` the following variable:

```
FEED_DEPLOYDIR_BASE_URI = http://<server-ip>:9999/ http://<server-ip>:9999/
```

Thus, our image will include all references to our package repository on our web server based on `busybox` (`httpd`), which is listening on port `9999`.

The second step is to create the package index on our repository:

```
$ source oe-init-build-env rpi-build
$ bitbake package-index
```

Apart from this, just create a web server listening on port 9999. The base directory will be the one where IPK packages are built. To make it easier to use the utility to connect `busybox`, use `httpd`(`http://wiki.openwrt.org/doc/howto/http.httpd`). It is also possible to use Apache, Nginx, or lighttpd. We can launch the `httpd` server with the following command:

```
$ cd rpi-build/tmp/deploy/ipk
$ busybox httpd -p 9999
```

To verify the proper operation of our package repository server, simply type `opkg` update from the Raspberry Pi:

```
$ opkg update
$ Downloading http://192.168.132.1:9999/....
```

 For further information, do not hesitate to visit `http://www.yoctoproject.org/docs/current/dev-manual/dev-manual.html#using-runtime-package-management`.

# Our application – an introduction

Now that we've covered how to generate the SDK for our platform and how to integrate package in our Yocto image, we will, through an example, develop an application with the **general purpose input output** (**GPIO**) pins of the Raspberry Pi and then create a recipe to integrate our application with the final image.

The idea is to develop an application that, through the GPIO pins, lights an LED and monitors a push button.

Here is the schematic diagram, realized with Fritzing (`http://fritzing.org/home/`):

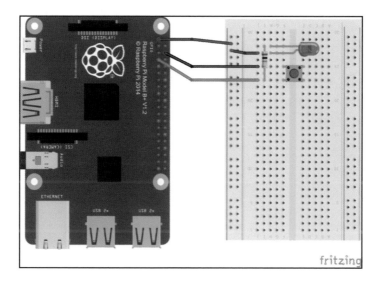

Thus, we can, from the Linux user space, light the LED or monitor the push button through GPIO 4 of the Raspberry Pi (pin 7 of the main connector).

We can test the following C application:

```
static int parse_opts(int argc, char *argv[])
int long_index = 0;
int opt;
static struct option option[]
{"Ied", required_argument, NULL, '1'
{"help", no_argument, NULL, 'h'
{"button", no_argument, NULL, 'b'
{"version", no_argument, NULL, 'v'
{0, 0, 0, 0
while ((opt = getopt_long(argc, argv, "Izbhv", option, &long_index)) >= 0)
switch(opt)
case 'h':
display_help(argv[0]);
exit(EXIT_SUCCESS);
case 'v':
fprintf(stderr, "\n%s - %s\n\n", project, VERSION);
exit(EXIT_SUCCESS);
case '1':
printf("Led Mode\n");
printf("Set gpio%d to %d\n",GPIO_PIN,atoi(optarg));
Set gpio4 to out mode
set_out(GPIO_PIN,atoi(optarg));
break;
case 'b':
printf("Button Mode\n");
Set gpio4 to in mode
set_in(GPIO_PIN);
wait_bp_state();
break;
default:
fprintf(stderr,"[ERROR] %s: Bad option. -h for help\n", argv[0]);
exit(EXIT_FAILURE);
return 0;
```

You can download it from the code bundle for this book.

We can try compiling our application with our SDK with the following command and send it to the Raspberry Pi:

```
$ source /opt/poky/1.7.1/environment-setup-armv6-vfp poky-linux- gnueabi
$ ${CC} gpio_example.c -o gpio_example
```

# Our application – creating the recipe

Now that our application is functional, we can create our recipe.

The first step is to create the file; for example, we can choose gpio-packt_0.1.bb.

- gpio-packt represents the name of the package (the PN variable).
- 0.1 represents the version number of the recipe (the PV variable).
- .bb represents the file extension (Bitbake).

The second step consists of placing the source code in a local repository, like this:

```
$ mkdir gpio-packt
$ cp /home/packt/gpio-example.c files/
$ ls gpio-packt
gpio-example.c
```

The recipe must be placed next to the gpio-packt directory, as shown here:

```
$ ls
gpio-packt/ gpio-packt.bb
```

After that, we can fill out our recipe like this:

```
DESCRIPTION = "gpio example"
LICENSE="GPLv2"
LIC_FILES_CHKSUM = "file://${COMMON_LICENSE_DIR}/GPL-
2.0;md5=801f80980d171dd6425610833a22dbe6"

PR = "r0"

SRC_URI = "file://gpio_example.c"

do_compile() {
        ${CC} ${CFLAGS} ${LDFLAGS} ${WORKDIR}/gpio_example.c -o
        gpio_example
}

do_install() {
        install -m 0755 -d ${D}${bindir}
        install -m 0755 ${S}/gpio_example ${D}${bindir}
}
```

# The recipe explained

Let's look at the various parts of the preceding recipe.

DESCRIPTION contains the description of the application. This information is used when the packet is generated so that the user can have this information through the package manager.

LICENSE contains the program license (GPLv2 in this example).

The LIC_FILES_CHKSUM variable contains checksums of the license text in the recipe source code. Poky uses this to track changes in the license text of the source code files.

PR contains the revision of the recipe used to build the package.

SRC_URI determines what files and source code are needed and where that source code should be obtained from (in this case, from the gpio-packt folder).

The `do_compile()` method will generate our binary that will be deployed on the Raspberry Pi.

The `do_install()` method will install our binary in the tree in the same way as installed on Raspberry Pi (in this case, the binary will be placed in `/usr/bin`).

The following table lists some paths used by Bitbake:

| | |
|---|---|
| base_bindir | /bin |
| base_sbindir | /sbin |
| base_libdir | /lib |
| datadir | /usr/share |
| sysconfdir | /etc |
| servicedir | /srv |
| bindir | /usr/bin |
| sbindir | /usr/sbin |
| libdir | /usr/lib |
| includedir | /usr/include |

Now that we have our recipe, we can include it in the image. To do this, we must put all files in the main tree. We will create a folder within `meta-raspberrypi/recipes-devtools`, as shown here:

```
$ cd meta-raspberrypi/recipes-devtools
$ mkdir gpio-packt-book
```

In order that Bitbake find our recipe, we can put the different files in this folder, like this:

```
$ cd gpio-packt-book
$ mv /home/packt/gpio-packt.bb
$ mv /home/packt/gpio-packt
```

The last step consists of integrating our recipe with the image. To do this, we can add the following variable to the `conf/local.conf` file:

```
IMAGE_INSTALL_append += " gpio-packt"
```

Now, we can launch Bitbake, and then test our program on the Raspberry Pi:

```
$ bitbake rpi-basic-image
```

The following commands to be executed on the Raspberry Pi.

You can test the LED with these commands:

```
$ gpio_example led=1 (set gpio4 to 1)
$ gpio_example led=0 (set gpio4 to 0)
```

You can use this command to test the button:

```
$ gpio_example --button
Button was pressed !
```

# Summary

In this chapter, we learned how to generate an SDK for the Raspberry Pi and how to manage packages, and we discovered how to deploy a custom application on the Raspberry Pi.

In the next chapter, you will be introduced to the layer concept, and you'll discover how to integrate another layer inside your environment of Yocto and Raspberry Pi.

# 6

# Working with External Layers

Throughout this chapter, we will discover the basic concept of external layers and understand layer types and how they are built (by priority, name, and so on). We will also discuss about the Qt5 and web server layers.

After that, we will integrate an external layer to our build and test it on the Raspberry Pi.

## Introducing layers

A layer is just a collection of recipes and/or configuration that can be used on top of Yocto/OE-Core.

The advantage of using an environment such as Yocto/OE (the Poky reference system) comes from the fact that this project handles a lot of metadata (definition files (`.conf`) of the machine (Raspberry Pi), classes, and recipes (`.bb`)) that covers everything from simple applications (`gpio-packt`) to graphics applications such as OpenGLES, EFL, or Qt.

The main motivation of using layers is to organize the long list of providers better and still make sure users may be able to pick only the required or desired provider. It is also a way of providing customizable source code that can be used for any architecture or modified in the way the user needs.

The other advantage is that we can choose all the layers required for each project (from the most basic to the most complex). We can modify them to be consistent with our architecture (ARM for the Raspberry Pi), but a layer can be reused on another architecture (PowerPC), and is it a big advantage in the industrial world (minimal effort is required when changing the architecture).

In addition, instead of redeveloping layers, always check whether the work has been done by others. It takes less time to download a layer providing a package we need and to add an append file (.bbapend); if some modifications are required, then you have to make them from scratch. To summarize, layers are added when needed.

You can find the different available layers at the following link:

`http://layers.openembedded.org/layerindex/branch/master/layers/`

# The basic concepts of layers

Let's dive into the basic concepts of layers:

## Theory

A layer, in the technical sense of the term, has some properties. They are as follows:

- **Name**: This usually starts with the string meta- (mandatory for better comprehension).
- **Priority**: This is the value used by BitBake to decide which recipe to use and the order in which the .bbappend files should be joined. It means that if two layers include the same recipe (.bb) file, the one with the higher priority is used.

For example, a layer with a priority value set to 6 has a higher chance of its recipe being used than one with a priority value set to 5.

Furthermore, each layer is listed according to its functionality on this page:

`http://layers.openembedded.org/layerindex/branch/master/layers/`

| | | | |
|---|---|---|---|
| meta-parallella | Support for the Parallella board from Adapteva | Machine (BSP) | https://github.com/nathanrossi/meta-parallella.git |
| meta-picosam9 | Picosam9 board support | Machine (BSP) | https://gitorious.org/picopc-tools/meta-picosam9.git |
| meta-qemu-bsps | layer for other qemu machines | Machine (BSP) | https://github.com/akuster/meta-qemu-bsps |
| meta-raspberrypi | Raspberry Pi board support | Machine (BSP) | git://git.yoctoproject.org/meta-raspberrypi |
| meta-renesas-rza1 | Official BSP layer for Renesas RZ/A1 platforms | Machine (BSP) | git://github.com/renesas-rz/meta-renesas-rza1 |
| meta-rockchip | Rockchip ARM hardware support | Machine (BSP) | git://github.com/linux-rockchip/meta-rockchip |
| meta-romley | Intel Romley platform BSP | Machine (BSP) | git://git.yoctoproject.org/meta-intel |
| meta-samsung | Samsung smartphone support | Machine (BSP) | git://github.com/shr-distribution/meta-smartphone.git |
| meta-sugarbay | Intel Sugar Bay platform BSP | Machine (BSP) | git://git.yoctoproject.org/meta-intel |

- **The software layer:** This layerprovides software families that can be used on any architecture (x86_64, ARM, PPC, MIPS, and so on). For example, we have meta-java (for Java support), meta-efl (for the Enlightenment environment), meta-qt5 (Qt support), meta-webserver (provides support for building web servers), meta-browser, and so on.
- **Miscellaneous**: If your layer doesn't fall into any other category, you can choose this type; however, there shouldn't be too many miscellaneous layers-it may be an indication that the purpose isn't well defined or that you should consider splitting the layer.
- **Machine (BSP):** These are layers specific to a machine (such as meta-raspberrypi, meta-fsl-arm, and meta-ti). They contain machine configuration files and recipes to configure packages for the machines.
- **Distribution**: These are layers adding a distribution to the environment (such as meta-ivito add in-vehicle infotainment (IVI) support, meta-angstrom, and so on).

At this stage, we know how the layers are distributed within the Yocto Project. Now, we will see how these layers are composed.

# The software layer

For this example, we will take as an example the `meta-qt5` layer. This layer has a directory tree, as follows:

```
pjtexier@amplitude:~ $ ls -l meta-qt5/
total 28
drwxrwxr-x  2 pjtexier pjtexier 4096 avril 22 19:20 classes
drwxrwxr-x  3 pjtexier pjtexier 4096 avril 22 19:20 conf
-rw-rw-r--  1 pjtexier pjtexier 1035 avril 22 19:20 COPYING.MIT
drwxrwxr-x  2 pjtexier pjtexier 4096 avril 22 19:20 licenses
-rw-rw-r--  1 pjtexier pjtexier 1189 avril 22 19:20 README
drwxrwxr-x  4 pjtexier pjtexier 4096 avril 22 19:20 recipes-devtools
drwxrwxr-x 10 pjtexier pjtexier 4096 avril 22 19:20 recipes-qt
```

# README and COPYING

Inside this directory, there are two important files; they are as follows:

- **README**: This file specifies mostly the outer layers that depend on the target layer, any configuration instructions, the address to send patches to, and contact details of the maintainers.
    - This layer depends on the following:

```
URI: git://github.com/openembedded/oe-core.git
branch: master
revision: HEAD

URI: git://github.com/openembedded/meta-oe.git
layers: meta-ruby
branch: master
revision: HEAD

When building stuff like qtdeclarative, qtquick, qtwebkit, make  sure
thatyou have required PACKAGECONFIG options enabled in qtbase build,  see
qtbase.inc  for detail.Send pull requests to openembedded-
devel@lists.openembedded.org  with '[meta-qt5]' in the subject'

When sending single patches, please using something like:
'git send-email -M -1 --to openembedded- devel@lists.openembedded.org --
subject-prefix=meta-qt5][PATCH'You are encouraged to fork the mirror on
github[1] to share your  patches. This is preferred for patch sets
consisting of more than one  patch. Other services like gitorious,
repo.or.cz or self hosted  setups  are of course accepted as well, 'git
fetch <remote>' works the same on  all of them. We recommend github because
```

it is free, easy to use, has  been proven to be reliable and has a really
good web GUI.1. https://github.com/meta-qt5/meta-qt5/

```
Main layer maintainers:
Martin 'JaMa' Jansa <martin.jansa@gmail.com>
Otavio Salvador <otavio@ossystems.com.br>
```

- **COPYING**: This file contains licensing information (MIT license in this case).

# The classes folder

The `classes` folder holds `.bbclass` files. Here is a sample `classes` folder:

```
pjtexier@amplitude:~ $ ls -l classes/
total 24
-rw-rw-r-- 1 pjtexier pjtexier 1721 avril 22 19:20 cmake_qt5.bbclass
-rw-rw-r-- 1 pjtexier pjtexier 2001 avril 22 19:20
populate_sdk_qt5.bbclass
-rw-rw-r-- 1 pjtexier pjtexier 7633 avril 22 19:20
qmake5_base.bbclass
-rw-rw-r-- 1 pjtexier pjtexier  219 avril 22 19:20 qmake5.bbclass
-rw-rw-r-- 1 pjtexier pjtexier 1935 avril 22 19:20
qmake5_paths.bbclass
```

# The conf folder

The `conf` folder should provide configuration (`.conf`) files. The `layer.conf` file inside
this folder contains some important variables, for example, the variable concerning the
priority (`BBFILE_PRIORITY`):

```
# Define the priority for recipes (.bb files) from this layer,
# choosing carefully how this layer interacts with all of the
# other layers.
BBFILE_PRIORITY_qt5-layer = "7"
```

To verify the priority value, we can use the following command:

```
$: bitbake-layers show-layers
```

## The recipes-* directory

The `recipes-*` directory contains some recipes. For example, in the meta-qt5 layer, we have `recipes-qt`, which include some metadata (such as Qt5).

## The machine (BSP) layer

For this presentation, we will take the example of the BSP layer specific to our hardware: the meta-raspberrypi BSP layer. This directory (folder) should contain a file list similar to the following:

```
pjtexier@amplitude:~ $ ls -l meta-raspberrypi/ classes
conf
custom-licenses
recipes-bsp
recipes-core
recipes-devtools
recipes-graphics
recipes-kernel
recipes-multimedia
COPYING.MIT
README
```

When we use a BSP layer, there are some differences. The first is in the `conf` folder. Now, we have a new folder inside this directory, which is `machine`.

This folder contains some configuration files to handle our specific hardware (Raspberry Pi and Raspberry Pi 2 among others). For example, there is an important file (`rpi-base.inc`) located at:

- machine

* `raspberry.conf` (configuration file for Raspberry Pi)

* `raspberry2.conf` (configuration file for Raspberry Pi2)

- Include

* rpi-base.inc

The `rpi-base.inc` file looks like this:

```
include conf/machine/include/rpi-default-settings.inc
include conf/machine/include/rpi-default-versions.inc
include conf/machine/include/rpi-default-providers.inc

SOC_FAMILY = "rpi"
include conf/machine/include/soc-family.inc

IMAGE_FSTYPES ?= "tar.bz2 ext3 rpi-sdimg"

SERIAL_CONSOLE = "115200 ttyAMA0"

XSERVER = " \
    xserver-xorg \
    xf86-input-evdev \
    xf86-input-mouse \
    xf86-input-keyboard \
    xf86-video-fbdev \
    "

# Really supported starting from linux-raspberrypi 3.18.y only
KERNEL_DEVICETREE ?= " \
    bcm2708-rpi-b.dtb \
    bcm2708-rpi-b-plus.dtb \
    bcm2709-rpi-2-b.dtb \
    \
    ds1307-rtc-overlay.dtb \
    hifiberry-amp-overlay.dtb \
    hifiberry-dac-overlay.dtb \
    hifiberry-dacplus-overlay.dtb \
    hifiberry-digi-overlay.dtb \
    iqaudio-dac-overlay.dtb \
    iqaudio-dacplus-overlay.dtb \
    lirc-rpi-overlay.dtb \
    pcf8523-rtc-overlay.dtb \
    pps-gpio-overlay.dtb \
    w1-gpio-overlay.dtb \
    w1-gpio-pullup-overlay.dtb \
    "
KERNEL_IMAGETYPE ?= "Image"

MACHINE_FEATURES = "kernel26 apm usbhost keyboard vfat ext2 screen
touchscreen alsa bluetooth wifi sdio"

# Raspberry Pi has no hardware clock
MACHINE_FEATURES_BACKFILL_CONSIDERED = "rtc"
```

```
MACHINE_EXTRA_RRECOMMENDS += " kernel-modules"

# Set Raspberrypi splash image
SPLASH = "psplash-raspberrypi"

IMAGE_BOOT_FILES ?= "bcm2835-bootfiles/*
${KERNEL_IMAGETYPE};${SDIMG_KERNELIMAGE}"
```

It is in this file that we set some essential variables, including the following:

- `SERIAL CONSOLE` specifies the speed and device for the serial console to attach to. It is passed to the kernel as a console parameter, for example, 115200 ttyAM0.
- `IMAGE FSTYPES` specifies the format of the root filesystem images to be created.
- `KERNEL IMAGETYPE` specifies the type of kernel image to build (uImage or zImage).

 If you want to know more about the BSP layer, you can visit `http://www.yoctoproject.org/docs/1.8/bsp-guide/bsp-guide.html`.

# Adding external layers to the Raspberry Pi

Now that we know how a layer works, we can add an existing external layer to our environment. To do this, we'll be working with meta-webserver (`http://layers.openembedded.org/layerindex/branch/master/layer/meta-webserver/`) in order to include the famous web server, **Monkey** (`http://monkey-project.com/`).

As you know, the first step consists of modifying our `conf/bblayers.conf` file in order to add the path of the layer, as follows:

```
# LAYER_CONF_VERSION is increased each time
build/conf/bblayers.conf
# changes incompatibly
LCONF_VERSION = "6"
BBPATH = "${TOPDIR}"
BBFILES ?= ""
BBLAYERS ?= " \
  /home/packt/RASPBERRYPI/poky/meta \
  /home/packt/RASPBERRYPI/poky/meta-yocto \
  /home/packt/RASPBERRYPI/poky/meta-yocto-bsp \
  /home/packt/RASPBERRYPI/poky/meta-raspberrypi \
```

```
    /home/packt/RASPBERRYPI/poky/meta-openembedded/meta-webserver \

    "
BBLAYERS_NON_REMOVABLE ?= " \
    /home/packt/RASPBERRYPI/poky/meta \
    /home/packt/RASPBERRYPI/poky/meta-yocto \
```

Now that we have included the layer so that BitBake can parse it, we can create our image with this command:

```
$ bitbake rpi-basic-image
```

At the end of the compilation/generation process, we can boot our Raspberry Pi and verify proper operation. To do this is very simple because we can just launch our favorite browser and type this in the address bar:

```
http://ip_address_of_rpi/2001
```

Now, we have an embedded web server on our Raspberry Pi. It is possible to create many projects using a simple web server (by upgrading firmware to make it fast) CGI, HTML5/JavaScript applications, applications with mpeg-streamer, and so on).

# Summary

In this chapter, we discovered the main principle of the layers inside the Poky distribution. We learned how a layer works, how to integrate an external layer to our Raspberry Pi projects, and how to generate a custom image.

We'll discuss layers in the next chapter as well, but we'll create our custom layer in order to integrate it to an image for the Raspberry Pi.

# 7

# Deploying a Custom Layer on the Raspberry Pi

In this chapter you will learn how to generate a custom layer with the different tools the Yocto Project offers. First of all, you'll discover how to generate a layer; then, you will integrate a recipe to the layer. In addition, to finish this chapter, we will generate a custom image. Reading this chapter will enable you to better organize your source code within the Yocto Project.

## Creating the meta-packt_rpi layer with the yocto-layer script

To create our custom layer, we can use two different methods:

- Manually: create the directory (meta-*) and create the layer configuration file (conf/layer.conf)
- * Use the yocto-layer script provided by the Poky environment

To gain flexibility and avoid mishandling, we'll use the second option. To use it, we must initially source all variables to gain access through our shell in the yocto-layerscript, as shown in the following command:

```
$ source oe-init-build-env rpi-build
```

Now that our environment is set up, we have access to the `yocto-layer` script, and so, we can begin the process of creating the layer.

Note that this script (`yocto-layer`) creates the layer in the current directory by default. That is why we must place it at the root of our environment:

```
$ cd /where/you/want/to/stored/your/layer
```

We can now launch the script using the following command:

```
$ yocto-layer create <layer_name> -o <dest_dir>
```

The **meta-string** is automatically prepended to the layer name.

For our example,we will call our layer **meta-packt_rpi**. Here is the command:

```
$ yocto-layer create packt_rpi
Please enter the layer priority you'd like to use for the layer: [default:
6]
Would you like to have an example recipe created? (y/n) [default: n]  y
Please enter the name you'd like to use for your example recipe: [default:
example] example-packt
Would you like to have an example bbappend file created? (y/n)  [default:
n] y
Please enter the name you'd like to use for your bbappend file:  [default:
example] example-packt
Please enter the version number you'd like to use for your bbappend  file
(this should match the recipe you're appending to): [default: 0.1]
New layer created in meta-packt_rpi.
Don't forget to add it to your BBLAYERS (for details see meta-
packt_rpi\README).
```

We have, through this script, generated our own layer, `meta-packt_rpi`, and inside this layer is a sample recipe, an example of `bbappend` file, and so on. An example of our generated layer is shown in the following command:

```
$ tree meta-packt_rpi/
meta-packt_rpi/
├── conf
│   └── layer.conf
├── COPYING.MIT
├── README
├── recipes-example
│   └── example
│       ├── example-packt-0.1
│       │   ├── example.patch
│       │   └── helloworld.c
│       └── example-packt_0.1.bb
└── recipes-example-bbappend
    └── example-bbappend
        ├── example-packt-0.1
        │   └── example.patch
        └── example-packt_0.1.bbappend
```

If we want to install our layer, we just have to integrate the absolute path inside the `bblayers.conf` file, as it says in the README file:

```
I. Adding the packt_rpi layer to your build
=====================================================
In order to use this layer, you need to make the build system aware  of it.

Assuming the packt_rpi layer exists at the top-level of your
yocto build tree, you can add it to the build system by adding the
location of the packt_rpi layer to bblayers.conf, along with any
other layers needed. e.g.:

  BBLAYERS ?= " \
    /path/to/yocto/meta \
    /path/to/yocto/meta-yocto \
    /path/to/yocto/meta-yocto-bsp \
    /path/to/yocto/meta-packt_rpi \
    "
```

We can add our layer to our `bblayers.conf` file:

```
# LAYER_CONF_VERSION is increased each time  build/conf/bblayers.conf
# changes incompatibly
LCONF_VERSION = "6"
BBPATH = "${TOPDIR}"
BBFILES ?= ""
BBLAYERS ?= " \
/home/packt/RASPBERRYPI/poky/meta \
/home/packt/RASPBERRYPI/poky/meta-yocto \
/home/packt/RASPBERRYPI/poky/meta-yocto-bsp \
/home/packt/RASPBERRYPI/poky/meta-raspberrypi \
/home/packt/RASPBERRYPI/poky/meta-openembedded/meta-webserver \
/home/packt/RASPBERRYPI/poky/meta-packt_rpi "
BBLAYERS_NON_REMOVABLE ?= " \
/home/packt/RASPBERRYPI/poky/meta \
/home/packt/RASPBERRYPI/poky/meta-yocto \
```

After this, our layer is fully integrated with the Yocto Project, and so, it can be parsed by BitBake (the meta scheduler).

> For further information, you can read the official documentation at
> `http://www.yoctoproject.org/docs/1.8/dev-manual/dev-manual.html#yocto-project-layers`.

# Adding gpio-packt to meta-packt_rpi

To test this layer, we will integrate the application developed in Chapter 5, *Creating, Developing, and Deploying on the Raspberry Pi* (`gpio-packt`). This will allow us to implement our layer step by step so that it is completely reusable for various projects. The hierarchy of your layer should look like this with the inclusion of this recipe:

```
$ tree meta-packt_rpi/
meta-packt_rpi/
├── conf
│   └── layer.conf
├── COPYING.MIT
├── README
├── recipes-custom
│   └── gpio-packt
│       ├── gpio-packt
│       │   └── gpio-example.c
│       └── gpio-packt.bb
├── recipes-example
│   └── example
│       ├── example-packt-0.1
│       │   ├── example.patch
│       │   └── helloworld.c
│       └── example-packt_0.1.bb
└── recipes-example-bbappend
    └── example-bbappend
        ├── example-packt-0.1
        │   └── example.patch
        └── example-packt_0.1.bbappend
```

As with any other extra package for our image, the build system needs to be aware that you want to include gpio-packt. For this purpose, edit your /conf/local.conf configuration file and add the following line to the bottom:

```
IMAGE_INSTALL_append = " gpio-packt"
```

This line tells the build system to include the gpio-packt package when creating the final image. If for some reason the variable already exists, just append the gpio-packt package name at the end, like this:

```
IMAGE_INSTALL_append = " app1 app2 gpio-packt"
```

Now, if we want to test it, we can launch BitBake with the following command and then test our program on the Raspberry Pi:

```
$ bitbake rpi-basic-image
```

# Patching gpio-packt

Now that we've seen how to integrate our recipe (gpio-packt) to the previously created layer (meta-packt_rpi), we will see how to create a patch to the gpio-packt recipe.

## Generating the patch

The first step is to create the .patch file. Use the following commands to create a backup of the original file:

```
$ cd meta-pack_rpi/recipe-custom/gpio_packt
$ cp gpio-packt/gpio-example.c gpio-packt/gpio-example.orig
```

Now, we can modify our main source code (gpio-example.c):

```
$ sed -i 's/Button Mode/Button Mode!/' gpio-packt/gpio-example.c
```

We have now changed our source file like we wanted to; the next step is to create our patch file with the diff command:

```
$ diff -u gpio-packt/gpio-example.orig gpio-packt/gpio-example.c >  gpio-packt/fix.patch
```

Now that we have our .patch file, we need to update our principal source file:

```
$ mv gpio-packt/gpio-example.orig gpio-packt/gpio-example.c
```

## Adding the patch to the recipe file

Be careful, because even if we have generated our .patch file, for now, it is still not visible because it has been entered in the SRC_URI variable. Here is the complete recipe,updated to take the patch into account:

```
DESCRIPTION = "gpio example"
LICENSE="GPLv2"
LIC_FILES_CHKSUM = "file://${COMMON_LICENSE_DIR}/GPL-
2.0;md5=801f80980d171dd6425610833a22dbe6"
```

```
PR = "r0"
SRC_URI = "file://gpio_example.c \
file://fix.patch\
"
do_compile() {
        ${CC} ${CFLAGS} ${LDFLAGS} ${WORKDIR}/gpio_example.c -o
gpio_example
}

do_install() {
        install -m 0755 -d ${D}${bindir}
        install -m 0755 ${S}/gpio_example ${D}${bindir}
}
```

If we take a look at the hierarchy of our layer, this is what we will see:

```
$ tree meta-packt_rpi/
meta-packt_rpi/
├── conf
│   └── layer.conf
├── COPYING.MIT
├── README
├── recipes-custom
│   └── gpio-packt
│       ├── gpio-packt
│       │   ├── fix.patch
│       │   └── gpio-example.c
│       └── gpio-packt.bb
├── recipes-example
│   └── example
│       ├── example-packt-0.1
│       │   ├── example.patch
│       │   └── helloworld.c
│       └── example-packt_0.1.bb
└── recipes-example-bbappend
    └── example-bbappend
        ├── example-packt-0.1
        │   └── example.patch
        └── example-packt_0.1.bbappend
```

Now, we can launch BitBake to test our new recipe with the following command:

```
$ bitbake rpi-basic-image
```

# Creating the raspberry-packt-image.bb image

Through out this chapter, our aim was to create a layer that can be reused in any environment. We'll see how to create our own image to be more dependent on images provided by the `meta-raspberrypi` BSP layer. There's no need to worry, because to create an image, we just need to make a recipe file.

## Creating the environment

To separate the recipes of our layer, we will position our image recipe in a layer called `recipe-core`, where we will create our `raspberry-packt-image.bb` recipe file. Here are the results of our layer after creating it:

```
$ tree meta-packt_rpi/
meta-packt_rpi/
├── conf
│   └── layer.conf
├── COPYING.MIT
├── README
├── recipes-core
│   └── images
│       ├── raspberry-packt-image.bb
├── recipes-custom
│   └── gpio-packt
│       ├── gpio-packt
│       │   ├── fix.patch
│       │   └── gpio-example.c
│       └── gpio-packt.bb
├── recipes-example
│   └── example
│       ├── example-packt-0.1
│       │   ├── example.patch
│       │   └── helloworld.c
│       └── example-packt_0.1.bb
└── recipes-example-bbappend
    └── example-bbappend
        ├── example-packt-0.1
```

```
|    └── example.patch
└── example-packt_0.1.bbappend
```

# Modifying the recipe file

To better manage our image, there's nothing better than to learn from the basic images contained in the `meta-raspberrypi` layer.

 You can visit the main GitHub repository at
`https://github.com/agherzan/meta-raspberrypi/blob/master/recipes-core/images/rpi-hwup-image.bb`.

Here is a basic example—our own image–compliant Raspberry Pi, including our own recipe:

```
# Base this image on core-image-minimal
include recipes-core/images/core-image-minimal.bb
DESCRIPTION = "Image for raspberry-pi"
IMAGE_FEATURES += "ssh-server-dropbear splash"
# Include modules in rootfs
IMAGE_INSTALL += " \
            kernel-modules \
            gpio-packt
            "
```

The `IMAGE_INSTALL` variable groups the related packages that generate our root filesystem. For further information, you can refer to the official documentation (`http://www.yoctoproject.org/docs/1.8/ref-manual/ref-manual.html#var-IMAGE_INSTALL`).

- Another variable that can be interesting, `IMAGE_FEATURES`, allows you to handle predefined packages (dev, debug, and so on). You can find more information by reading the official documentation:

- **allow-empty-password:** Allows Dropbear and OpenSSH to accept root logins and logins from accounts having an empty password string.

- **dbg-pkgs:** Installs debug symbol packages for all packages installed in a given image.

- **debug-tweaks:** Makes an image suitable for development (e.g. allows root logins without passwords and enables post-installation logging). See the 'allow-empty-password', 'empty-root-password', and 'post-install-logging' features in this list for additional information.

- **dev-pkgs:** Installs development packages (headers and extra library links) for all packages installed in a given image.

- **doc-pkgs:** Installs documentation packages for all packages installed in a given image.

- **empty-root-password:** Sets the root password to an empty string, which allows logins with a blank password.

- **package-management:** Installs package management tools and preserves the package manager database.

- **post-install-logging:** Enables logging postinstall script runs to the `/var/log/postinstall.log` file on first boot of the image on the target system.

- **ptest-pkgs:** Installs ptest packages for all ptest-enabled recipes.

- **read-only-rootfs:** Creates an image whose root filesystem is read-only. See the "Creating a Read-Only Root Filesystem" section in the Yocto Project Development Manual for more information.

- **splash:** Enables showing a splash screen during boot. By default, this screen is provided by `psplash`, which does allow customization. If you prefer to use an alternative splash screen package, you can do so by setting the `SPLASH` variable to a different package name (or names) within the image recipe or at the distro configuration level.

- **staticdev-pkgs:** Installs static development packages, which are static libraries (i.e. `*.a` files), for all packages installed in a given image.

- For example, in our example (`raspberry-pack-image.bb`), we used several packages through IMAGE_FEATURES, such as splash and ssh-server-dropbear.

We have also used this variable (in Chapter 5, *Creating, Developing, and Deploying on the Raspberry Pi*) in `conf/local.conf` in order to add the `package-management` package (with EXTRA_IMAGE_FEATURES).

Another example of IMAGE_FEATURES is if we want to work with the integration of the Eclipse IDE, we have to add the following package to the `conf/local.conf` file:

```
IMAGE_FEATURES += "eclipse-debug"
```

# Deploying the raspberry-packt-image.bb image

Now comes the time when we can test our image and check its operation. To do this, we have to launch usual `bitbake` command, but this time with an argument-the name of our image, `raspberry-packt-image`:

```
$ bitbake raspberry-packt-image
Loading cache: 100%
|#####################################################################
#####################################################################
#################| ETA:  00:00:00
```

Now, we have a 100% custom environment (`layer`, `recipe`, and `image`).

> Remember, to learn how to best handle the `meta-packt_rpi` layer directory, you can visit
> `http://www.yoctoproject.org/docs/1.4.2/dev-manual/dev-manual.html#managing-layers`.

# Summary

In this chapter, we learned how to generate a custom layer using the `yocto-layer` script. We also learned how to integrate a recipe into this, and finally, we created a custom image and it on our Raspberry Pi.

In the next chapter, we will explore all of the Raspberry Pi's peripherals.

# 8

# Diving into the Raspberry Pi's Peripherals and Yocto Recipes

In this chapter, we will learn how to handle the SPI and i2c buses of the Raspberry Pi through the Yocto Project. We'll see how to write our own recipe for custom applications.

## The SPI bus

The **Serial Peripheral Interface** (**SPI**) protocol implements a synchronous serial link between a master and a slave. When a single slave is used, only three signals (and ground) are needed.

The master generates an **SCLK** (serial clock) clock signal, which is sent to the slave. On some transitions of this clock, the slave will read data using the appointed signal, **MOSI** (short for master out, slave in), or write it using the signal named **MISO** (master in, slave out). There are several names, depending on hardware manufacturers, used to describe these signals. It is recommended to use the MISO/MOSI notation (the most common one), because it removes any ambiguity: the MOSI pin of a master must always be connected to the MOSI pin of a slave, and the same is true for the MISO pin.

If several slaves are to be connected to the same host, they may be connected in parallel (all MISO pins connected together as well as all MOSI pins), but an additional signal (**CS**, or Chip Select) is required for each of them, to choose which pin communication is established with at a given time. An example is presented in the following figure:

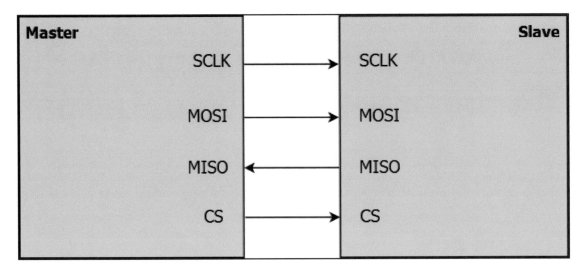

Have fun with the SPI protocol on your Raspberry Pi; we will explore it further through a utility developed for our platform.

 For further information about the SPI protocol, you can visit the following website:
`https://en.wikipedia.org/wiki/Serial_Peripheral_Interface_Bus`

# The spi-tools project

To quickly establish a connection with an SPI device from a shell script, for example, we suggest you use a small package that a French engineer (Christophe Blaess) has recently developed, which simplifies configuration and bidirectional communication. It is a free project called **spi-tools**.

This project is divided into two tools:

- **spi-config**: This allows you to view or edit the communications settings on a an SPI port. Here is the command:

  ```
  $ spi-config
  ```

- **spi-pipe**: This allows full-duplex talk with a device by redirecting standard input and standard output to the specified SPI port. The command is as follows:

  ```
  $ spi-pipe
  ```

> If you want more information, consult the readme file in the GitHub repository: `https://github.com/cpb-/spi-tools`

# Inclusion in the meta-oe layer

The advantage of spi-tools is that it has been completely integrated into the Yocto/OE environment since April 2015. Indeed, it is part of the meta-oe layer.

> You can look at the initial commit here:
> `https://github.com/openembedded/meta-oe/commit/90b13eded7`
> `6f7f7fa1a6715e67c32504e7788e96`

It is easy to introduce this layer to our environment in order to use these utilities. Here we see another advantage of the Yocto Project: flexibility.

If you want to visit the metadata index of this recipe, you can visit `http://layers.openembedded.org/layerindex/recipe/33576/`.

As you may have guessed, the first step in integrating the spi-tools recipe is modifying our `conf/bblayers.conf` file in order to add the path of the layer:

```
# changes incompatibly
LCONF_VERSION = "6"
BBPATH = "${TOPDIR}"
BBFILES ?= ""
BBLAYERS ?= " \
  /home/packt/RASPBERRYPI/poky/meta \
  /home/packt/RASPBERRYPI/poky/meta-yocto \
  /home/packt/RASPBERRYPI/poky/meta-yocto-bsp \
  /home/packt/RASPBERRYPI/poky/meta-raspberrypi \
  /home/packt/RASPBERRYPI/poky/meta-packt_rpi \
  /home/packt/RASPBERRYPI/poky/meta-openembedded/meta-oe \ "
BBLAYERS_NON_REMOVABLE ?= " \
  /home/packt/RASPBERRYPI/poky/meta \
  /home/packt/RASPBERRYPI/poky/meta-yocto \
```

 You can downloaded the `meta-oe` layer by using this following command:

```
$ git clone https://github.com/openembedded/meta- openembedded.git
```

Now that the path of our layer has been set, it is visible to BitBake and spi-tools can be integrated with our root filesystem. To do this, we need to run the command to create the binaries.

# Baking spi-tools

In order to generate the package (`ipk`, `rpm`, or `dpkg`), we can run the following command:

```
$ bitbake spitools
Loading cache: 100%
|###############################################################
###############################################################
###################| ETA:  00:00:00
Loaded 2006 entries from dependency cache.
NOTE: Resolving any missing task queue dependencies
Build Configuration:
BB_VERSION        = "1.27.1"
BUILD_SYS         = "x86_64-linux"
NATIVELSBSTRING   = "Ubuntu-14.04"
TARGET_SYS        = "arm-poky-linux-gnueabi"
MACHINE           = "raspberrypi"
```

```
DISTRO            = "poky"
DISTRO_VERSION    = "1.8+snapshot-20150729"
TUNE_FEATURES     = "arm armv6 vfp arm1176jzfs callconvention-hard"
TARGET_FPU        = "vfp"
meta
meta-yocto
meta-yocto-bsp    = "master:19f77cf586fbee9e67d3698263402b717303c5ec"
meta-raspberrypi  = "master:7457bf182c8fd550ec877ecd786a3edd16e65495"
meta-packt_rpi    = "master:19f77cf586fbee9e67d3698263402b717303c5ec"
meta-oe           = "master:f637fadb106a09a6f3dfba4181d06dc9b5e82ff5"
NOTE: Executing SetScene Tasks
NOTE: Executing RunQueue Tasks
Currently 1 running tasks (373 of 381):
0: spitools-git-r0 do_configure (pid 3535)
```

Alternatively, if we want to integrate spi-tools into our image, we just have to add the following line to our image and run BitBake `raspberry-pack-image`:

```
# Base this image on core-image-minimal
include recipes-core/images/core-image-minimal.bb
DESCRIPTION = "Image for raspberry-pi"
IMAGE_FEATURES += "ssh-server-dropbear splash"
# Include modules in rootfs
IMAGE_INSTALL += " \
    kernel-modules \
    gpio-packt     \
    spitools       \
    "
```

# Testing on the Raspberry Pi

With our image in hand, we can now run the utilities offered by spi-tools.

## spi-config

To access SPI interfaces from user space, the kernel provides us entry points as special files in /dev. This requires the loading of the following module:

```
$ modprobe spidev
```

After integrating this module, we can try to launch the `spi-config` utility:

```
$ spi-config
spi-config: no device specified (use option -h for help)
$ spi-config -h
usage: ./spi-config options...
      options:
          -d --device=  use the given spi-dev character device.
          -q --query         print the current configuration.
          -m --mode=[0-3]    use the selected spi mode.
                    0: low iddle level, sample on leading edge
                    1: low iddle level, sample on trailing edge
                    2: high iddle level, sample on leading edge
                    3: high iddle level, sample on trailing edge
          -l --lsb={0,1}     LSB first (1) or MSB first (0)
          -b --bits=[7...]   bits per word
          -s --speed=   set the speed in Hz
          -h --help          this screen
          -v --version       display the version number
```

For example, if we wanted to query the /dev/spidev0.0 interface, we would run this:

```
$ spi-config -d /dev/spidev0.0 -q
/dev/spidev0.0: mode=0, lsb=0, bits=8, speed=500000
```

 If you want more details about `spi-config`, you can visit
https://github.com/cpb-/spi-tools/blob/master/src/spi-config.c.

# spi-pipe

The **spi-pipe** program can send the data it receives from its standard input to the SPI **MOSI** line, while simultaneously displaying data received from the **MISO** SPI line on its standard output.

The general principle of operation is as follows:

```
$ <command-1> | spi-pipe [options] | <command-2>
```

For example, if we want to send some data to another SPI peripheral, we can use the following command:

```
$ printf "HELLO from R-pi" | spi-pipe -d /dev/spidev0.0 | hexdump -C
```

 Note that the three members of a pipeline run in parallel, each in a separate process, by synchronizing the data that flows between them.

## Conclusion

Finally, here is a selection of the various applications for which these tools can be used:

Communicating with a microcontroller to retrieve data from an ADC

Communicating with an SPI flash

Communicating with a delay line

We leave it up to you to think of other types of applications.

## The i2c bus

The i2c protocol enables us to port a master component (usually the microprocessor) and several slave devices. Several masters can share the same bus, and the same component can send slave status to the master or vice versa. However, communication takes place only between the master and one slave. Note also that the master can send a command to all slaves simultaneously (such as a sleep or reset request).

At the electrical level, the protocol uses signals alternating between high and low levels; the most common value pairs are (0, 5V) and (0, 3.3V). The SCL clock signal is generated by the master. The serial data (SDA) data signal is set high or low by the master or slave, according to the communication phase. Throughout the duration of the high segment of the **SCL** clock, the **SDA** data signal must be kept high or low, depending on whether it transmits a 1 or a 0.

Finally, as shown in the following figure, particular configurations of signals (produced by the master) can indicate the beginning or end of an exchange, which are called the **START** and **STOP** conditions. This is a variation of the **SDA** signal for a slot clock.

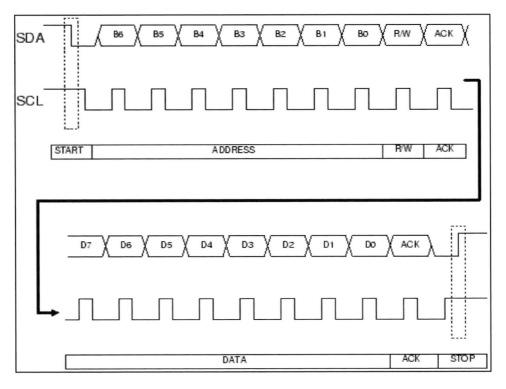

In order to test the i2c interface on our Raspberry Pi, we will develop an application to retrieve data from a Wii Nunchuck through the i2c bus.

# The Wii Nunchuck

The Nunchuck has an X/Y joystick, an X/Y/Z accelerometer, and two buttons (Z and C).

The sensor data is communicated through the i2c bus.

# The Nunchuck connector

The connector contains four wires, two of which are power and ground. The other wires are used for i2c communication (SDA and SCL). The following diagram demonstrates the principle:

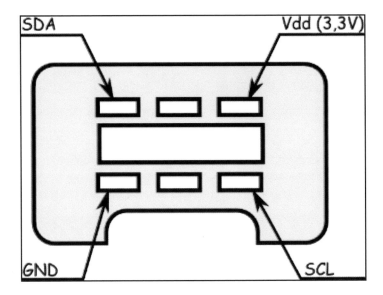

 If you are worried about your connection, you can find an adapter for this controller at `https://www.sparkfun.com/products/9281`.

# The Raspberry Pi connection

For the connection with our Raspberry Pi, we just have to connect it to the main connectors, **I2C1_SDA** and **I2C1_SCL**, as shown in this pin diagram:

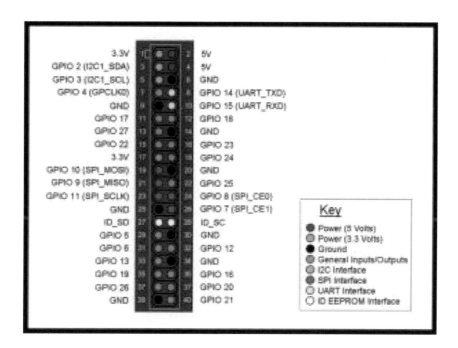

# The Nunchuck's protocol

The Wii Nunchuck contains a controller that communicates through the i2c bus. In order to know where to store bytes written to it, the first byte must be an 8-bit register address. In other words, each `write()` operation to the Nunchuck requires one register address byte, followed by data bytes.

For a write operation, the first byte sent to the Nunchuck tells it where to start (the START condition).

# Encryption

The Nunchuck is designed to provide a specific encrypted link. However, this can be disabled through the following process:

- Write 0x55 to the Nunchuck's 0xF0 register
- Pause
- Write 0x00 to the Nunchuck's 0xFB register

| Write | Pause | Write | | | |
|-------|-------|-------|------|------|
| 0xF0 | 0x55 | – | 0xFB | 0x00 |

Note that if you own a white Nunchuck, the process will be different:

- Write 0x00 to the Nunchuck's 0x40 register

| Write | |
|-------|------|
| 0x40 | 0x00 |

Once this has been successfully performed, all data is returned unencrypted.

# Requesting sensor data

The whole point of us using the Nunchuck is to read its sensor data. When requested, it should return six bytes of data, formatted as follows:

| Data byte receive | | | | | | | | Address |
|---|---|---|---|---|---|---|---|---|
| Joystick X | | | | | | | | 0x00 |
| Joystick Y | | | | | | | | 0x01 |
| Accelerometer X (bit 9 to bit 2 for 10-bit resolution) | | | | | | | | 0x02 |
| Accelerometer Y (bit 9 to bit 2 for 10-bit resolution) | | | | | | | | 0x03 |
| Accelerometer Z (bit 9 to bit 2 for 10-bit resolution) | | | | | | | | 0x04 |
| Accel. Z bit 1 | Accel. Z bit 0 | Accel. Y bit 1 | Accel. Y bit 0 | Accel. X bit 1 | Accel. X bit 0 | C-button | Z-button | 0x05 |

The following table illustrates the message sequence:

| Write | Pause | Read | | | | | |
|-------|-------|------|---|---|---|---|---|
| 0x00 | – | 1 | 2 | 3 | 4 | 5 | 6 |

# Testing the i2c connection

You can start automatically detecting connected devices with **i2cdetect**. i2cdetect is not installed on the Raspberry Pi; the easiest method of using it is to install the i2c-tools package through our `raspberry-packt-image` Yocto image by adding **i2c-tools**, as follows:

```
# Base this image on core-image-minimal
include recipes-core/images/core-image-minimal.bb
DESCRIPTION = "Image for raspberry-pi"
IMAGE_FEATURES += "ssh-server-dropbear splash"
# Include modules in rootfs
IMAGE_INSTALL += " \
    kernel-modules \
    gpio-packt    \
    spitools      \
    i2c-tools     \
    "
```

After that, we can launch the BitBake raspberry-pack-image command to test it on the Raspberry Pi.

In order to detect the i2c device, we just have to launch the following commands on the Raspberry Pi:

```
$ modprobe i2c-dev
$ i2cdetect 0
WARNING! This program can confuse your I2C bus, cause data loss and worse!
I will probe file /dev/i2c-0.
I will probe address range 0x03-0x77.
Continue? [Y/n] Y
     0  1  2  3  4  5  6  7  8  9  a  b  c  d  e  f
00:          03 04 05 06 07 -- -- -- -- -- -- -- --
10: -- -- -- -- -- -- -- -- -- -- -- -- -- -- -- --
20: -- -- -- -- -- -- -- -- -- -- -- -- -- -- -- --
30: -- -- -- -- -- -- -- -- -- -- -- -- -- -- -- --
40: -- -- -- -- -- -- -- -- -- -- -- -- -- -- -- --
50: -- -- 52 -- -- -- -- -- -- -- -- -- -- -- -- --
60: -- -- -- -- -- -- -- -- -- -- -- -- -- -- -- --
70: -- -- -- -- -- -- -- --
```

If the Nunchuck is working, it will show up in the display at address `0x52`.

 The Nunchuck uses the i2c address 0x52. If you want more information about the i2c interface on the Raspberry Pi, you can visit `https://learn.adafruit.com/adafruits-raspberry-pi-lesson-4-gpio-setup/configuring-i2c`.

# Creating the Nunchuck application

We can now test our Nunchuck application (developed in the C language). You will find it in the code bundle that came with this book.

We can test compiling our application with our SDK with the following command and send it to the Raspberry Pi:

```
$ source /opt/poky/1.7.1/environment-setup-armv6-vfp poky-linux- gnueabi
$ ${CC} nunchuck.c -o nunchuck_packt
```

# Integrating with meta-packt_rpi

Now, we will prepare our environment so that all of our development is Yocto compliant.

Here is our custom integration layer for the Nunchuck recipe:

```
$ tree meta-packt_rpi/
meta-packt_rpi/
├── conf
│   └── layer.conf
├── COPYING.MIT
├── README
├── recipes-core
│   └── images
│       └── raspberry-packt-image.bb
├── recipes-custom
│   ├── gpio-packt
│   │   ├── gpio-packt
│   │   │   ├── fix.patch
│   │   │   └── gpio_example.c
│   │   └── gpio-packt_0.1.bb
│   └── nunchuck
│       ├── nunchuck
│       │   └── nunchuck.c
│       └── nunchuck_0.1.bb
├── recipes-example
```

```
|   └── example
|        ├── example-packt-0.1
|        │    ├── example.patch
|        │    └── helloworld.c
|        └── example-packt_0.1.bb
└── recipes-example-bbappend
    └── example-bbappend
         ├── example-packt-0.1
         │    └── example.patch
         └── example-packt_0.1.bbappend
```

The `nunchuck_0.1.bb` file will contain the recipe for implementing the Nunchuck binary in our rootfs.

# Creating the Nunchuck recipe

Now that our application is functional, we can create our recipe so that BitBake can find it.

Here is the recipe that enables us to integrate the Nunchuck application into the Raspberry Pi:

```
DESCRIPTION = "nunchuck i2c example"
LICENSE="GPLv2"
LIC_FILES_CHKSUM = "file://${COMMON_LICENSE_DIR}/GPL
2.0;md5=801f80980d171dd6425610833a22dbe6"
PR = "r0"
SRC_URI = "file://nunchuck.c"
S = "${WORKDIR}"
do_compile() {
        ${CC} ${CFLAGS} ${LDFLAGS} ${WORKDIR}/nunchuck.c -o
nunchuck_packt
}
do_install() {
        install -m 0755 -d ${D}${bindir}
        install -m 0755 ${S}/nunchuck_packt ${D}${bindir}
}
```

To integrate the package into the Raspberry Pi environment, we have to add the following line to `raspberry-pack-image`:

```
# Base this image on core-image-minimal
include recipes-core/images/core-image-minimal.bb
DESCRIPTION = "Image for raspberry-pi"
IMAGE_FEATURES += "ssh-server-dropbear splash"
# Include modules in rootfs
IMAGE_INSTALL += " \
```

```
    kernel-modules \
    gpio-packt     \
    i2c-tools      \
    spitools       \
    nunchuck       \
    "
```

# Testing the Nunchuck application

Now, we can launch BitBake and test our program on the Raspberry Pi. Use this command:

```
$ bitbake raspberry-packt-image
```

On the Raspberry Pi, launch the following command:

```
$ nunchuck
```

You can now have fun with Nunchuck and Video4Linux (V4L).

Next, will see how to integrate video support to our environment.

# V4L presentation

V4L is a video API for Linux. It is integrated into the Linux kernel. It is an abstract layer between video software and video devices. It allows the capture of video streams and pictures from digital camcorders, video capture cards, TV and radio tuners, webcams, and so on.

For example, it is possible to work with OpenCV (to retrieve the video stream through /dev/video) and Qt to display content (using a framebuffer or X11).

# Video support

In order to add video support, we need only look at the readme file of our BSP layer (meta-raspberry-pi). It will be evident that we can easily add video support:

```
2.F. Optional - Video camera support with V4L2 drivers
    =======================================================
Set this variable to enable support for the video camera (Linux 3.12.4+
required)
VIDEO_CAMERA = "1"
```

The VIDEO_CAMERA variable must be set in conf/local.conf.

# v4l-utils integration

In order to control the device connected to /dev/videoX, there is a set of utilities called v4l-utils. The integration of these tools is easy, as usual, through our build system (Yocto/OpenEmbedded).

To integrate the v4l-utils package to the Raspberry Pi environment, we have to add the following line to raspberry-pack-image:

```
# Base this image on core-image-minimal
include recipes-core/images/core-image-minimal.bb
DESCRIPTION = "Image for raspberry-pi"
IMAGE_FEATURES += "ssh-server-dropbear splash"
# Include modules in rootfs
IMAGE_INSTALL += " \
    kernel-modules \
    gpio-packt    \
    i2c-tools     \
    spitools      \
    nunchuck      \
    v4l-utils     \
    "
```

After that, we just have to launch the following command:

```
$ bitbake rapberryrapberry-packt-image
Loading cache: 100%
|##################################################################
###################################################################
##################| ETA:   00:00:00
Loaded 2057 entries from dependency cache.
NOTE: Resolving any missing task queue dependencies
Build Configuration:
BB_VERSION        = "1.27.1"
BUILD_SYS         = "x86_64-linux"
NATIVELSBSTRING   = "Ubuntu-14.04"
TARGET_SYS        = "arm-poky-linux-gnueabi"
MACHINE           = "raspberrypi"
DISTRO            = "poky"
DISTRO_VERSION    = "1.8+snapshot-20150804"
TUNE_FEATURES     = "arm armv6 vfp arm1176jzfs callconvention-hard"
TARGET_FPU        = "vfp"
meta
meta-yocto
```

```
meta-yocto-bsp      = "master:19f77cf586fbee9e67d3698263402b717303c5ec"
meta-raspberrypi    = "master:7457bf182c8fd550ec877ecd786a3edd16e65495"
meta-packt_rpi      = "master:19f77cf586fbee9e67d3698263402b717303c5ec"
meta-oe
meta-multimedia     = "master:f637fadb106a09a6f3dfba4181d06dc9b5e82ff5"
NOTE: Preparing RunQueue
NOTE: Executing SetScene Tasks
NOTE: Executing RunQueue Tasks
Currently 1 running tasks (558 of 566):
0: v4l-utils-1.6.2-r0 do_configure (pid 20717)
```

Once the process is complete, it will be possible to use `v4l-utils`.

 If you want more information about `v4l-utils`, you can visit `http://www.linux-projects.org/modules/sections/index.php?op=viewarticle&artid=16`.

# Summary

In this chapter, we learned how to integrate a package to test the SPI interface of the Raspberry Pi. We also learned how to create an application for the Wii Nunchuck and how to deploy it inside the Yocto Project.

In the next chapter, we will understand how to integrate a media hub with the Raspberry Pi.

# 9
# Making a Media Hub on the Raspberry Pi

In this chapter, we will learn how to deploy a custom application in order to make an embedded media hub (panel control for temperature, ADC, serial, and so on).

We will work on aspects of rpm packages, init scripts, recipes, and web development.

## Project description – CPU temperature monitoring

The idea of this project is the creation of a web interface that allows, for example, monitoring of the CPU temperature.

To do this, we will use technologies such as **HTML5** and **nodejs**. We will also have utilities available on the Raspberry Pi, such as **vcgencmd**.

In this project, we will use technical aspects, such as:

- Websocket
- Justgage
- Nodejs

The idea here is not to explain these technologies, but to learn that they can be used in the Yocto Project.

# Overview

The following diagram represents the project's structure:

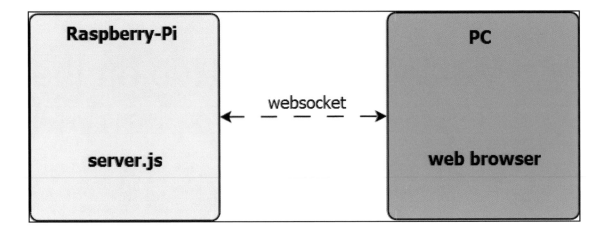

## Hardware/software requirements

You'll need the following hardware and software for this project:

- A Raspberry Pi
- A host PC
- An SD card
- SSH/SCP

# Creating the main application

The main project contains several files. To best present things, we'll only concentrate on two files:

- `server.js`: This is the file that will create our web server and send data to the HTML web page
- `index.html`: This is the page that will open the web browser to display the data received

# server.js

The `server.js` file creates a server on the listening port `3344` and will be responsible for creating a socket (`rpi_temperature`) that contains the CPU temperature of Raspberry Pi. The socket function uses, among others, the `vcgencmd` command (`https://github.com/raspberrypi/firmware/blob/master/opt/vc/bin/vcgencmd`), permitting us to monitor the CPU temperature, as shown here:

```
setInterval(function()
{
    child = exec("vcgencmd measure_temp | awk -F:", function        (error,
stdout, stderr)
    {
        if (error !== null)
        {
            console.log('exec error: ' + error);
        }
        else
        {
            var date = new Date().getTime();
            var temp = parseFloat(stdout);
            socket.emit('rpi_temperature', date,temp);
        }
    }
);}, 1000);
```

 For further information about `vcgencmd`, you can visit the following page: `http://elinux.org/RPI_vcgencmd_usage`

# index.html

Here is an example of a function receiving the socket (`rpi_temperature`) containing the CPU temperature of our Raspberry Pi:

```
$(document).ready(function(){
    socket.on('rpi_temperature', function (time, data) {
      gg1.refresh($.trim(data));
      return false;
    });
});
```

# Creating the Yocto/OE environment

Now that we have developed the main application, what remains for us is to integrate it with our Yocto RPI environment.

## Modifying the image

The first step consists of integrating the `nodejs` package (located at `meta-openembedded/meta-oe/recipes-devtools/nodejs`) with the Raspberry Pi environment. For this, we have to add the following line to `raspberry-pack-image`:

```
# Base this image on core-image-minimal
include recipes-core/images/core-image-minimal.bb
DESCRIPTION = "Image for raspberry-pi"
IMAGE_FEATURES += "ssh-server-dropbear splash"
# Include modules in rootfs
IMAGE_INSTALL += " \
    kernel-modules \
    gpio-packt    \
    i2c-tools     \
    spitools      \
    nunchuck      \
    v4l-utils     \
    nodejs        \
"
```

We have now integrated `nodejs` with our Poky distro.

## Creating the recipe file

The second step consists of creating the recipe file; let's call this recipe `webserver-packt_01.bb`.

The idea is to have the following architecture inside the `recipes-custom` folder:

```
$ tree webserver-packt/
webserver-packt/
├── webserver-packt
│   └── server.tar.gz
└── webserver-packt_0.1.bb
```

> The `server.tar.gz` tarball contains the main application (nodejs + HTML5).

To create this recipe, we will use the `recipetool` command , as follows:

```
$ source oe-init-build-env rpi-build
$ recipetool create -d -o webserver-packt_0.1.bb ../meta-
packt_rpi/recipes-custom/webserver-packt/webserver-packt/
$ cp webserver-packt_0.1.bb ../meta-packt_rpi/recipes-custom/webserver-
packt/
```

> The complete documentation of `recipetool` command is online at
> `http://www.yoctoproject.org/docs/1.8/mega-manual/mega-man`
> `ual.html#new-recipe-creating-the-base-recipe-using-`
> `recipetool`.

Now we just need to copy the entire archive (`server.tar.gz`) containing the sources to `${datadir}` (`/usr/share/`); this step is carried out in the `do_install()` block, as shown here:

```
DESCRIPTION = "Panel to monitor rpi temperature"
LICENSE = "GPLv2"
LIC_FILES_CHKSUM =
"file://${COREBASE}/meta/COPYING.GPLv2;md5=751419260aa954499f7abaabaa882bbe
"

# Package Release
PR = "r0"

# Use local tarball
SRC_URI = " \
  file://server.tar.gz \
  "
RDEPENDS_${PN} += "bash"

# Make sure our source directory (for the build) matches the directory
structure in the tarball
```

```
S = "${WORKDIR}"

do_install() {
  install -d ${D}${datadir}/server-packt
  cp -a ${S}/server ${D}${datadir}/server-packt
}

# Package files
FILES_${PN} += "${datadir}/server-packt"
```

# Explanation

Let's take a look at what the variables do:

- The `RDEPENDS_{PN}` variable lists a package's runtime dependencies that must be installed in order for the built package to run correctly. In our case, bash is necessary for `nodejs`.
- * The `FILES_{PN}` variable contains the list of directories or files that are placed in the packages. In our case, `server-packt` is necessary.

We now have an environment ready to be used. If we want to deploy the application on our Raspberry Pi, we can do so with the following commands.

The host commands are as follows:

```
$ bitbake webserver-packt
$ scp tmp/deploy/rpm/arm1176jzfshf_vfp/webserver-packt-0.1-
r0.arm1176jzfshf_vfp.rpm  root@ip_address_of_rpi:/home/
```

These are the Raspberry Pi commands:

```
$ rpm -ivh webserver-packt-0.1-r0.arm1176jzfshf_vfp.rpm
$ rm webserver-packt-0.1-r0.arm1176jzfshf_vfp.rpm
$ node /usr/share/server-packt/server/server.js
```

# Autostarting – the init file

If we want to have a standalone application, it would be interesting if our application can start during the boot sequence of our Raspberry Pi. For this, we will use an `init` script, inheriting directly from System V.

The first step is to create a `.init` file within our structure. We will call this file `server.init`. The tree will look like this:

```
$ tree webserver-packt/
webserver-packt/
├── webserver-packt
│   ├── server.init
│   └── server.tar.gz
└── webserver-packt_0.1.bb
```

So, the script will start the application automatically after the installation and every time the Raspberry Pi starts up. Here is the `init` script from System V:

```
#!/bin/bash
### BEGIN INIT INFO
# Provides:           server.init
# Required-Start:     $remote_fs $syslog
# Required-Stop:Å     $remote_fs $syslog
# Default-Start:      2 3 4 5
# Default-Stop:       0 1 6
# Short-Description:  Start daemon at boot time
# Description:        Enable service provided by daemon.
### END INIT INFO

DAEMON=node
NAME=server.init
DESC="Nodejs app"
ARGS="/usr/share/server-packt/server/server.js"

set -e

usage()
{
        echo "---------------------------------"
        echo "Usage: $0 (stop|start|restart)"
        echo "---------------------------------"
}

service_start()
{
    echo -n "starting $DESC: $NAME... "
```

```
        start-stop-daemon -S -x $DAEMON -- $ARGS &
        echo "done."
}


echo ""
service_stop()
{
    echo -n "stopping $DESC: $NAME... "
    start-stop-daemon -K -x $DAEMON
    echo "done."
}
case $1 in
        stop)
                service_stop
                echo ""
        ;;
        start)
                service_start
                echo ""
        ;;
        restart)
                service_stop
                service_start
                echo ""
        ;;
        *)
                usage
esac
exit 0
```

# Explanation

Let's look at how the code works:

- The DAEMON variable specifies the binary to launch (/usr/bin/node)
- The NAME variable specifies the script name
- The DESC variable contains some information about DAEMON (node)
- The ARGS variable contains the arguments to pass to DAEMON (node)

If you want to test this script on the Raspberry Pi, use these commands:

```
$ scp server.init root@ip_address_of_rpi:/etc/init.d
$ cd /etc/init.d
$ update-rc.d server.init defaults
```

This command stops the application:

```
/etc/init.d/server.init stop
```

This one restarts it:

```
/etc/init.d/server.init restart
```

# Autostarting – the recipe file

The inclusion of our init file in our webserver-packt.bb recipe consists of:

- Adding the server.init file to SRC_URI.
- Adding do_install() to the step for our init script.
- Including update-rc.d. Adding this to Yocto is done by adding inherit update-rc.d to our recipe.

Here is webserver-packt.bb after being updated:

```
DESCRIPTION = "Panel to monitor rpi temperature"
LICENSE = "GPLv2"
LIC_FILES_CHKSUM =
"file://${COREBASE}/meta/COPYING.GPLv2;md5=751419260aa954499f7abaabaa882bbe
"

# Package Release
PR = "r0"

# Use local tarball
SRC_URI = " \
    file://server.tar.gz \
    file://server.init \
    "
RDEPENDS_${PN} += "bash"

# Make sure our source directory (for the build) matches the directory
structure in the tarball
S = "${WORKDIR}"
```

```
do_install() {
    install -d ${D}${datadir}/server-packt
    cp -a ${S}/server ${D}${datadir}/server-packt
    install -d ${D}${sysconfdir}/init.d/
    install -m 0755 ${WORKDIR}/server.init ${D}${sysconfdir}/init.d/server-
packt-init
}

# Package files
FILES_${PN} += "${datadir}/server-packt"

inherit update-rc.d

INITSCRIPT_NAME = "server-packt-init"
INITSCRIPT_PARAMS = "start 99 5 2 . stop 19 0 1 6 ."
```

# Explanation

Here is an explanation of our updated `webserver-packt.bb` file:

- The `INITSCRIPT_NAME` variable represents the filename of the initialization script, as installed to `/etc/init.d`.
- * The `INITSCRIPT_PARAMS` variable specifies the options to pass to `update-rc.d`. In our case, the script has a `runlevel` of `99`, is started at init levels 2 and 5, and is stopped at levels 0, 1, and 6.

 If you want more information about `update-rc.d`, you can visit the official documentation of the Yocto Project:
`http://www.yoctoproject.org/docs/1.8/mega-manual/mega-man`
`ual.html#ref-classes-update-rc.d`

# Deploying raspberry-packt-image

Now that we have a functional application (`webserver-packt`), we can add it to our custom image, `raspberry-pack-image`:

```
# Base this image on core-image-minimal
include recipes-core/images/core-image-minimal.bb
DESCRIPTION = "Image for raspberry-pi"
·IMAGE_FEATURES += "ssh-server-dropbear splash"
# Include modules in rootfs
IMAGE_INSTALL += " \
```

```
kernel-modules \
gpio-packt     \
i2c-tools      \
spitools       \
nunchuck       \
v4l-utils      \
nodejs         \
webserver-packt \
"
```

After doing this, we can start creating our image and then mount it on an SD card:

```
$ bitbake raspberry-packt-image
```

# Testing the application

In order to test the application on the Raspberry Pi, you have just to go to the following address from your favorite browser:

```
http://raspberry-pi-ip-address:3344
```

If the whole environment has been properly configured, you should see the following page:

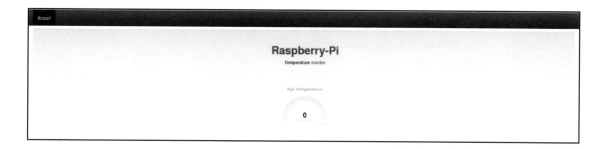

# The future of this project

We looked at the basic idea of a server, and you should be able to improve it in order to make it as industrial as possible. One can easily imagine the following applications:

- Monitoring the ADCs, present on a motherboard
- Sending serial commands to a device via an HTML page (node-serial)
- Monitor a CAN-bus devices (`https://github.com/sebi2k1/node-can`)

The final project might look something like this:

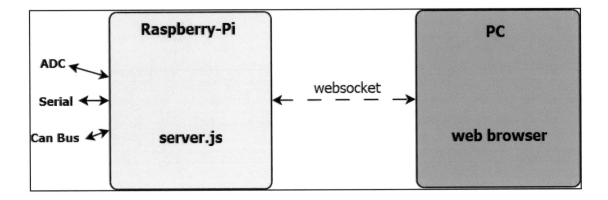

# Summary

In this chapter, we learned how to create a web interface, how to integrate it within an existing environment, and how to deploy it on the Raspberry Pi.

In the next chapter we will learn some basics about the Linux kernel and how to configure the kernel to support various LCD touchscreens. Further on the chapter explains how to setup a Yocto project to run graphical applications or a window system, on a Raspberry Pi using a LCD touchscreen.

# 10
## Playing with an LCD Touchscreen and the Linux Kernel

When setting up an LCD touchscreen using an embedded Linux system, it's recommended to have basic knowledge of the Linux kernel and how to configure it. In this chapter, we will learn some basics about the Linux kernel and how to download, configure, and compile it using a cross compiler. The current recommendation when running a Linux-based system on the Raspberry Pi is to use the Raspberry Pi Linux kernel instead of the the mainline Linux kernel; we will learn why in this chapter.

Later in the chapter, we will go through how to boot an image based on the Yocto Project with a windowing system using a Raspberry Pi 7 touchscreen and a PiTFT 2.8 touchscreen. The chapter will end with a walkthrough of how to use the Qt application framework to develop graphical applications for the Raspberry Pi that are possible to play using a touchscreen.

## The Linux kernel

The Linux kernel is a Unix-like operating system kernel created by Linus Torvalds 1991. It was originally developed for 32-bit x86-based PCs, but today, Linux also supports a large set of architectures such as ARM, PowerPC, MIPS, and SPARC. The Linux kernel is a fundamental part of a Linux distribution (such as Ubuntu, Debian, and Fedora).

When deciding which kernel is most suited to your project, it's good to have in mind how kernel releases work. Depending on your needs, you can choose between **mainline**, **developing**, or **stable** kernels. If you don't work with kernel development, it's recommended to avoid using the mainline kernel since it's still under development and is considered unstable. A kernel is always considered stable directly after it has been released from the mainline tree. After that, the kernel will be maintained until the next mainline kernel becomes available (usually in 2-3 months). However, a kernel can be picked as a longterm kernel, which means that it will be maintained for an extended period (several years). Longterm kernels are often used in commercial projects, since these projects require a stable and supported base that can have important bug and security fixes backported for a long time.

Visit `https://www.kernel.org/releases.html` for more details about kernel releases.

# The Linux kernels versus the Raspberry Pi Linux kernel

The currently recommended kernel for the Raspberry Pi is the official Raspberry Pi Linux kernel (`https://github.com/raspberrypi/linux.git`). The reason we need a specific kernel for the Raspberry Pi (instead of using the mainline Linux kernel) is mainly the proprietary firmware/GPU binary blob needed by the Raspberry Pi. However, in 2014, the full documentation for the VideoCore IV graphics core, together with the complete source for the graphics stack, was released by Broadcom, under a three-clause BSD license. This lead to the gap between the mainline support for bcm2835 (the SoC used in the Raspberry Pi) and the support for the Rasbberry Pi Linux kernel decreasing significantly. With that said, there is still some hard work left to do in the mainline kernel, for example, video decoding and camera support. Also, some important drivers such as the rpi-ft5406 (used for the official Raspberry Pi touchscreen) still don't exist within the mainline Linux kernel.

Read more about the current status of the Raspberry Pi kernel upstreaming to the mainline kernel at `http://elinux.org/RPi_Upstreaming`.

# Getting started with the Linux kernel

In this part of the chapter, we will go through how to download, configure, and compile a custom Linux kernel.

Different mainline versions of the kernel can be downloaded from **kernel.org,** either as an archived file or through GitHub. In the examples, we will use version 4.1 of the kernel, since its currently the default in `meta-raspberrypi`. You can easily find the default version for `meta-raspberrypi` by searching for `PREFERRED_VERSION_linux-raspberrypi`, like this:

```
$ cd meta-raspberrypi
$ git grep PREFERRED_VERSION_linux-raspberrypi
conf/machine/include/rpi-default- versions.inc:PREFERRED_VERSION_linux-
raspberrypi ?= "4.1.%"
```

Start by downloading the kernel and then go to the 4.1 branch:

```
$ cd /path/to/workdir
$ git clone
https://git.kernel.org/cgit/linux/kernel/git/stable/linux-stable.git/
$ git checkout -b linux-4.1.y -t remotes/origin/linux-4.1.y
```

Remember that when building for the Raspberry Pi, `https://github.com/raspberrypi/linux.git` is the supported kernel repository. Use it like this:

```
$ git clone https://github.com/raspberrypi/linux.git
$ git checkout -b rpi-4.1.y -t remotes/origin/rpi-4.1.y
```

Next, we can start working with our kernel. First, we need to decide what configuration to use; all existing configurations exist under `arch/*/configs/` in the kernel tree. Later, we will look at how to make our own customizations to the kernel, but for now, we will start by using a predefined configuration for the ARM platform. When building from your host machine, you need to set up a cross compiler for the ARM architecture, which in this case is bcm2835 (which happens to be the CPU family of the Raspberry Pi). Use this command:

```
$ make O=/path/to/output_dir  CROSS_COMPILE=/path/to/arm-linux-gnueabi-
ARCH=arm bcm2835_defconfig
    make[1]: Entering directory '/path/to/output_dir'
      HOSTCC   scripts/basic/fixdep
      GEN      ./Makefile
      HOSTCC   scripts/kconfig/conf.o
      SHIPPED  scripts/kconfig/zconf.tab.c
      SHIPPED  scripts/kconfig/zconf.lex.c
      SHIPPED  scripts/kconfig/zconf.hash.c
      HOSTCC   scripts/kconfig/zconf.tab.o
      HOSTLD   scripts/kconfig/conf
    #
    # configuration written to .config
    #
    make[1]: Leaving directory '/path/to/output_dir'
```

The command will ensure that the chosen configuration, a makefile, and a symlink to the original source tree are stored in the output directory. It's not mandatory to use an output directory; you can build directly within the kernel tree itself. However, it's strongly recommended to specify an output directory to avoid problems in your main kernel tree and keep it clean from build results. Next, we can start building the kernel. If building from a multi-core machine, it's recommended to use the `-j` flag in order to speed up the build.

```
$ make O=/path/to/output_dir CROSS_COMPILE=/path/to/arm-linux-gnueabi-
ARCH=arm -j4
    make[1]: Entering directory `/path/to/output_dir''
      GEN      ./Makefile
    scripts/kconfig/conf  --silentoldconfig Kconfig
    make[1]: Leaving directory `/path/to/output_dir''
    make[1]: Entering directory `/path/to/output_dir''
      CHK      include/config/kernel.release
      GEN      ./Makefile
      WRAP     arch/arm/include/generated/asm/bitsperlong.h
      WRAP     arch/arm/include/generated/asm/cputime.h
      WRAP     arch/arm/include/generated/asm/current.h
    ...
      OBJCOPY arch/arm/boot/zImage
      Kernel: arch/arm/boot/zImage is ready
    make[1]: Leaving directory `/path/to/output_dir'
```

If you want to change the configuration of your kernel, a predefined target called `menuconfig` can be used. It will give you a menu that contains entries for all the configurable parts of your kernel. It's possible to search for keywords in the menu to find a requested configuration option; this can be achieved by typing / followed by the keyword. Typing ? in the menu will display a short description of the configuration option you selected.

```
make O=/path/to/output_dir  CROSS_COMPILE=/path/to/arm-linux-gnueabi-
ARCH=arm menuconfig
```

Here is an example of using `menuconfig`. The M symbol means that the driver will be built as a separate module that can be loaded/unloaded by the kernel on demand.

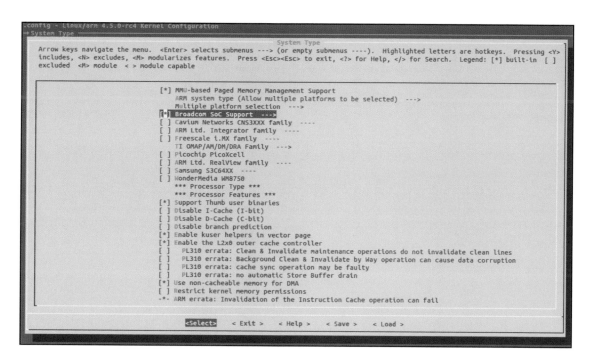

When the new configuration has been saved, you can build the kernel in the same way as described earlier in the chapter.

# Configuring the kernel in Yocto

When using Yocto, it's possible to use BitBake for configuring and compiling the kernel. The following example will show you how to perform these steps in the Yocto Project, using the Raspberry Pi kernel as an example:

```
$ cd /path/to/project
$ bitbake linux-raspberrypi -c menuconfig
```

Perform your modifications and save the new `defconfig`, and then run this command:

```
$ bitbake linux-raspberrypi
```

As described in earlier chapters of this book, these commands will set up the cross compiler for you under the hood. In the Yocto Project, it's possible to take a customized kernel configuration file (`.config`) and put it into the kernel recipe. Then, you will have to name it `defconfig` and point it out in the `SRC_URI` variable for the recipe. This will cause the kernel to be built using the `defconfig` file as the default configuration. It's also possible to use a feature called **fragments**, which makes it possible to add a fragment of the kernel configuration options in a file called `<somename>.cfg`. When added to the `SRC_URI` variable, it will update the kernel configuration with the information from the fragment. For `linux-raspberrypi` (the kernel recipe in `meta-raspberrypi`), it's not possible to use defconfig or fragments, since it takes the kernel configuration directly from the kernel repository (`bcmrpi_defconfig` or `bcm2709_defconfig`) and overrides the `defconfig` file. In order to change kernel configuration options for `meta-raspberrypi`, a couple of possibilities exist. The first option is to create an integration patch for the kernel that modifies the the chosen `defconfig` file within the kernel tree and is then applied through the kernel recipe, like this:

```
diff --git a/recipes-kernel/linux/linux-raspberrypi_4.1.bb b/recipes-
kernel/linux/linux-raspberrypi_4.1.bb
index 3a3cf40..bddf79b 100644
--- a/recipes-kernel/linux/linux-raspberrypi_4.1.bb
+++ b/recipes-kernel/linux/linux-raspberrypi_4.1.bb
@@ -1,6 +1,8 @@
 LINUX_VERSION ?= "4.1.10"
 SRCREV = "b74df9228c27f55361c065bc5dbfba88861cc771"
-SRC_URI =
"git://github.com/raspberrypi/linux.git;protocol=git;branch=rpi-4.1.y"
+SRC_URI =
"git://github.com/raspberrypi/linux.git;protocol=git;branch=rpi-4.1.y \
+            file://0001-bcmrpi_defconfig-add-debug.patch \
+            "
```

Another option is to use the `kernel_configure_variable` function from `linux.inc` in `meta-raspberrypi` and then prepend the configuration of the kernel recipe using this function:

```
diff --git a/recipes-kernel/linux/linux.inc b/recipes-
kernel/linux/linux.inc
index fae78b7..12eec7e 100644
--- a/recipes-kernel/linux/linux.inc
+++ b/recipes-kernel/linux/linux.inc
@@ -107,6 +107,8 @@ do_configure_prepend() {
    # Activate CONFIG_LEGACY_PTYS
    kernel_configure_variable LEGACY_PTYS y
+   kernel_configure_variable TOUCHSCREEN_STMPE y
+

    # Keep this the last line
    # Remove all modified configs and add the rest to .config
    sed -e "${CONF_SED_SCRIPT}" < '${WORKDIR}/defconfig' >> '${B}/.config'
```

# Configuring the kernel with LCD support

When using an LCD display with your Raspberry Pi, your kernel must fulfill some requirements in order to ensure that the display is fully functional. First of all, you need to know whether the kernel you want to use supports your display. Using an old kernel version with a brand new display is often problematic since the drivers required for your display didn't exist when the old kernel was developed, and new drivers are seldom backported to older kernel versions. This leaves you with two choices. The first is doing the hard work of trying to backport the requested drivers by yourself. This is very difficult and often hard to achieve even for an experienced kernel developer, depending on how old kernel is that the backport is needed for. The other, more suitable, solution is to use a newer kernel version with the drivers for your display included.

Even if your kernel contains all the parts needed to get your display up and running, you have to ensure that all drivers are enabled. Starting from kernel version 3.18, Raspberry Pi has official support for something called a device tree, which can be used to simplify the configuration of the kernel.

In this subsection, we will go through these topics:

- The device tree: What is it and how to use it on the Raspberry Pi
- The configuration of a touchscreen from the kernel perspective: How to configure the kernel on the Raspberry Pi to handle different touchscreens

# The Raspberry Pi device tree

A **device tree** (**DT**) is a tree data structure that contains a description of the device's hardware. A DT can manage resource allocation and handle module loading, which eases problems with drivers competing for system resources. For the ARM architecture, **device tree source** (**DTS**) files are stored within the kernel tree under /arch/arm/boot/dts. When the kernel is build, the DTS files are compiled into **device tree blobs** (**DTBs**). To be able to use DTs, both the firmware and kernel must support it, since the bootloader will be responsible for loading the DTB along with the kernel (the third-stage bootloader, start.elf, will pass the device tree blob to the Raspberry Pi).

The Raspberry Pi uses its GPU (VideoCore IV) to boot the system. It starts by loading its first-stage bootloader. This will make it possible to access and run the second-stage bootloader, bootcode.bin (located on the SD card). The second-stage bootloader is executed on the GPU and will load the third-stage bootloader, called start.elf. The main responsibilities of the third-stage bootloader are to read and parse configurations and pass them to the GPU and kernel, together with loading the kernel image. The bootcode.bin and start.elf bootloaders, together with the configuration (such as cmdline.txt and config.txt), are located on the SD card.

Passing a DTB to a kernel that 'doesn't support device trees will prevent the image from booting. In order to handle this in a generic way, a trailer added by the mkknlimg tool is used by the bootloader to check whether the kernel supports DT.

The management of device tree is done using the config.txt file for the Raspberry Pi. The base device trees are located in the **/boot** partition alongside start.elf and are named bcm*-rpi-b[-plus].dtb (the A and A+ models are compatible and are supposed to use B and B+ device tree's). An example from config.txt of enabling the i2c interface, adding HiFiBerry support, and ensuring that the base DT for the Raspberry Pi B+ is loaded can be seen here:

```
dtparam=i2c=on
dtoverlay=bcm2708-rpi-b-plus
dtoverlay=hifiberry-dacplus
```

When using the latest firmware, the loader will, based on your hardware, try to load one of the base device trees by default without the need for you to specify it in config.txt.

# Configuring the touchscreen from the kernel perspective

In this subsection, we will go through the basic kernel configuration needed for the PiTFT 2.8 touchscreen and the Raspberry Pi 7 touchscreen.

First, we need to choose what configuration we should use for our base. When using `meta-raspberrypi`, this will be handled automatically by the build system after we have specified either `raspberrypi` or `raspberrypi2` as our `MACHINE` variable in `local.conf`. When using a custom kernel, we need to know which existing configuration is suitable for our Raspberry Pi model. Currently, there are three choices: `bcmrpi_defconfig` (first-generation Raspberry Pi), `bcm2709_defconfig` (second-generation Raspberry Pi), or `bcm2835_defconfig` (only fully supported in later kernel versions). In our example, we will be using a Raspberry Pi 2. When the configuration has been decided, we can start by doing a basic configuration of the kernel, as shown here:

```
$ cd /path/to/rpi_kernel_repo
$ mkdir -p /path/to/output_dir
$ O=/path/to/output_dir  CROSS_COMPILE=/path/to/arm-linux-gnueabi- ARCH=
bcm2709_defconfig
```

Using BitBake and `meta-raspberrypi`, you need to do the following:

```
$ bitbake linux-raspberrypi -c configure
```

 For a custom kernel, the `config` will be stored at `/path/to/kernel_output/.config`. When using Yocto and meta-raspberrypi, it will be stored at `./tmp/work/raspberrypi*-poky-linux-gnueabi/linux-raspberrypi/<kernel_version_and_revision>/linux-raspberrypi*-standard-build/.config`.

Once we have our basic configuration in place, we can check whether it contains the most basic configurations required for bringing up our display. Note that the following configurations are currently enabled by default in the Raspberry Pi configurations.

For PiTFT 2.8, these options must be enabled:

```
CONFIG_INPUT_TOUCHSCREEN=y
CONFIG_OF_TOUCHSCREEN=y
CONFIG_TOUCHSCREEN_STMPE=m
CONFIG_FB_TFT_FBTFT_DEVICE=m
```

Besides the generic touchscreen support configuration, we need to ensure that the stmpe and fbtft devices are built. The stmpe_ts device is needed to get working touch functionality for the PiTFT. The fbtft device is a framebuffer driver for small TFT LCD displays, such as the PiTFT's. The device supports the use of SPI and GPIO, which are used by PiTFT displays, and will ensure that the display is registered and noticed by the kernel. Besides these options, basic setup of SPI and i2c is required to get everything up and running.

In this book, we will assume the usage of a kernel version with device tree support for Raspberry Pi (kernel 3.18+). This means that we need to modify config.txt to make sure that required parts are automatically loaded using device trees, like this:

```
dtparam=spi=on
dtparam=i2c1=on
dtparam=i2c_arm=on
dtoverlay=pitft28r,rotate=90,speed=32000000,fps=20
```

For the official Raspberry Pi 7, it's enough to enable the following:

```
CONFIG_INPUT_TOUCHSCREEN=y
CONFIG_OF_TOUCHSCREEN=y
CONFIG_TOUCHSCREEN_RPI_FT5406=m
```

Then, enable ft5406 overlay in config.txt:

```
dtoverlay=rpi-ft5406
```

We have learned what basic configuration is needed for the kernel to be functional with some common touchscreen models for the Raspberry Pi. In the next section, we will learn how these parts, together with required userspace settings, can be set up using the Yocto Project.

# Setting up an LCD display for the Raspberry Pi using the Yocto Project

There exist a number of different LCD displays for the Raspberry Pi. Among the most popular are the official Raspberry Pi 7 touchscreen and the PiTFT displays (often called PiTFT Hats, since they are suitable to mount on top of the Raspberry Pi). For now, we will focus on the Raspberry Pi 7 touchscreen and the PiTFT models.

In this section, we will go through how to boot a standard Yocto Project image, containing a window system and a working touchscreen.

## The Raspberry Pi 7 touchscreen

Getting started with the Raspberry Pi 7 touchscreen using an image based on the Yocto Project requires quite a few configurations. First, we need to ensure we are using a 4.1+ kernel. Starting from the **jethro** release of meta-raspberrypi, 4.1 is the default version. Currently, meta-raspberrypi lacks full support for the Raspberry Pi 7 touchscreen, so we need to perform some small modifications before booting our image.

 Build instructions for the Raspberry Pi 7 touchscreen can be found at `https://www.adafruit.com/images/product-files/2718/2718bu ild.jpg`. The display will work with Raspberry Pi A/B boards; however, the mounting holes on the back of the display will only line up with A+, B+, and Raspberry Pi 2/3.

If using the default meta-raspberrypi settings, we will have a supported kernel with all the required configuration options enabled by default. To be extra safe, you can go through the previous part of this chapter to ensure that the kernel is correctly configured for your display. With this in mind, we can start by creating a new project:

```
$ source /path/to/poky/oe-init-build-env my_project
```

Next, we can continue with the normal procedure and add external layers required for building Raspberry Pi images with Yocto:

```
$ cat local/bblayers.conf
# LAYER_CONF_VERSION is increased each time build/conf/bblayers.conf
# changes incompatibly
LCONF_VERSION = "6"
BBPATH = "${TOPDIR}"
BBFILES ?= ""
BBLAYERS ?= " \
        /path/to/poky/meta \
        /path/to/poky/meta-yocto \
        /path/to/poky/meta-yocto-bsp \
        /path/to/meta-raspberrypi \
        /path/to/meta-openembedded/meta-oe \
        /path/to/meta-openembedded/meta-multimedia \
"
BBLAYERS_NON_REMOVABLE ?= " \
        /path/to/poky/meta \
        /path/to/poky/meta-yocto \
```

If you haven't cloned the openembedded layers for the earlier examples in the book, it can be done with this command:
**$ git clone git://git.openembedded.org/meta-openembedded**

We also need to make some modifications to `local.conf`:

```
$ echo "MACHINE = "raspberrypi"" >> conf/local.conf (Or
MACHINE=raspberrypi2)
$ echo "LICENSE_FLAGS_WHITELIST = "commercial"" >> conf/local.conf
```

After this, we are ready to start a new build. By default, meta-raspberrypi will ensure that, for example, input devices for the touchscreen, together with appropriate udev rules, are set up for the touchscreen. These settings will be applied seamlessly during the build:

```
$ bitbake core-image-sato
```

Once the SD card has been prepared with the new image, we also need to ensure that all required drivers are loaded for the touchscreen. This can be done by adding this line to the end of `config.txt`, which is located in the boot partition of the SD card:

```
$ echo "dtoverlay=rpi-ft5406" >> /path/to/sdcard/boot/config.txt
```

Now, you're ready to rock and will be able to boot a window system with touch support using your Raspberry Pi 7 touchscreen.

A Raspberry Pi 7 touchscreen running `core-image-sato`

# The PiTFT 2.8 resistive touchscreen

Native support for PiTFT displays in meta-raspberrypi is fairly new. Check whether your PiTFT model is supported by looking at the readme file for meta-raspberrypi, under the Enable PiTFT support section"".

PiTFT support is configurable for any existing (or customized) Raspberry Pi image using the Yocto Project. The support has been added as MACHINE_FEATURES in meta-raspberrypi. The MACHINE_FEATURES variable is a standard Yocto Project feature, which can be used to add hardware features for the target your are building for. There exists a set of predefined MACHINE_FEATURES features in the Yocto Project, which includes Wi-Fi, keyboard, Alsa, and Bluetooth, among others. In the Raspberry Pi BSP layer, a couple of these are enabled by default:

```
$ grep "MACHINE_FEATURES " conf/machine/include/rpi-base.inc
MACHINE_FEATURES += "kernel26 apm usbhost keyboard vfat ext2 screen
touchscreen alsa bluetooth wifi sdio"
```

PiTFT support will require two new `MACHINE_FEATURES` features: a generic one called **pitft** and a model-specific version. In this example, we will be using **pitft28r**, which corresponds to the PiTFT 2.8 resistive touchscreen. The simplest way to add the new `MACHINE_FEATURES` features is by adding them to the local configuration file within your project:

```
$ cd /path/to/my/rpi/project
$ echo "MACHINE_FEATURES += "pitft pitft28r"" >> conf/local.conf
```

This will add support for either running a console-based image or a window-system image. The pitft feature will, under the hood, ensure that SPI and i2c are enabled. It will also configure the framebuffer for handling the PiTFT display (change from `/dev/fb0` to `/dev/fb1`). The model-specific machine feature (pitft28r in this example) will add the model-specific device tree overlay to `config.txt`, set up proper configurations for the screen (such as orientation and speed), and ensure that the stmpe module needed for the touch functionality is loaded. It will also add some default calibration data for the touchscreen. When the `MACHINE_FEATURES` features are set up, we can build our image, load it on the SD card, and boot:

```
$ bitbake core-image-sato
```

The PiTFT 2.8 resistive touchscreen running core-image-sato

When you boot your Raspberry Pi, the LCD will turn white at first. After a short while, it should turn black again-this means that the kernel has recognized the screen. Shortly after, you should be up and running with a window system. The 2.8"" screen is quite small, but it's possible to use the virtual keyboard in order to write, for example, simple commands in the terminal. The touchscreen has been calibrated for you using default values, suitable for your screen and rotation. If you find the default calibration insufficient, for example, if you wish to change the display orientation (90 degrees by default), you can recalibrate it using, for example, `ts_calibrate`.

> `ts_calibrate` is part of the `tslib` recipe in Poky. It's included by default when `building core-image-sato`, and it can easily be added to a custom image by specifying `MACHINE_FEATURES += "touchscreen"`

# Developing applications and using them on an LCD display

At this point, we have an image based on the Yocto Project with PiTFT display support up and running on our Raspberry Pi. In this section, we will develop a graphical application that we can use with our fancy touchscreen. When developing graphical applications, a couple of different frameworks exist. Qt is one of the most famous graphical frameworks for embedded devices and exists in a free software version. In this section, we will go through how to set up and develop a graphical application for embedded Linux environments using Qt and EGLFS. Qt is a cross-platform application framework, so besides being able to run on various types of hardware, it can also be used in many different software platforms (such as X11, OS X, Windows, and EGLFS). EGLFS, which we will be using in our example, is basically a platform plugin used for running Qt applications on top of EGL and OpenGL ES. In fact, it will not even require a window system (such as X11) to work, which makes it highly suitable for embedded Linux.

# Developing a custom application using Qt

When developing an application based on Qt using the Yocto Project, we need to set up Qt in our layer. Two standard methods exist for developing a graphical application: either build your application against an exported SDK, or create a new recipe for your application. In this example, we will develop our application against an exported SDK. To succeed with getting our new application to build and run on the target, we need to perform these steps.

- Add the external layers required for Qt
- Export the SDK containing Qt support
- Create the Qt application and build it against the exported SDK
- Set up an image with Qt support for the target
- Run Qt applications on the official Raspberry Pi 7"" touchscreen

There exist a number of different Qt versions, where Qt5 is the latest. We will use the meta-qt5 external layer when developing our new application. First, we need to download meta-qt5 and enable the usage of it in our project:

```
$ git clone https://github.com/meta-qt5/meta-qt5.git
```

Add meta-qt5 to local/bblayers.conf:

```
$ cat local/bblayers.conf
# LAYER_CONF_VERSION is increased each time build/conf/bblayers.conf
# changes incompatibly
LCONF_VERSION = "6"

BBPATH = "${TOPDIR}"
BBFILES ?= ""

BBLAYERS ?= " \
  /path/to/poky/meta \
  /path/to/poky/meta-yocto \
  /path/to/poky/meta-yocto-bsp \
  /path/to/meta-raspberrypi \
  /path/to/meta-openembedded/meta-multimedia \
  /path/to/meta-qt5 \
  "
BBLAYERS_NON_REMOVABLE ?= " \
  /path/to/poky/meta \
  /path/to/poky/meta-yocto \
```

Next, we need to export the SDK and unpack it to a preferred location:

```
$ bitbake meta-toolchain-qt5
$ ./tmp/deploy/sdk/poky-glibc-x86_64-meta-toolchain-qt5-cortexa7hf-vfp-
vfpv4-neon-toolchain-2.0.1.sh
```

The path might be different, depending on which model of the Raspberry Pi and which release of the Yocto Project you are using.

> If you are unsuccessful with building meta-toolchain-qt5, you can try to build it without the X11 and Wayland packages. Using X11 and Wayland together with qt5 has been been problematic at times when using meta-raspberrypi. Use this command: **$ echo "DISTRO_FEATURES_remove = "x11 wayland"" >> conf/local.conf.**
> If you still have problems building, include the meta-packt-qt5 layer and try again. The layer contains some workarounds for qt5 on Raspberry Pi. Refer to the `readme` file within the layer for additional information.

Set up the environment for using the cross compiler:

```
$ cd /path/to/extracted_sdk
$ source environment-setup-cortexa7hf-vfp-vfpv4-neon-poky-linux-gnueabi
$ which qmake
/path/to/extracted_sdk/sysroots/x86_64-pokysdk-linux/usr/bin/qt5/qmake
```

Once the SDK is in place and we have set up the cross compiler, we are ready to build our first Qt application for the Raspberry Pi. The first example is a simple Qt application based on C++ that contains some clickable widgets. When building a Qt application from the command line, **qmake** can be used to create a project and generate the makefile, like so:

```
$ tar -zxf qt_packtpub_app.tar.gz
$ cd qt_packtpub_app
$ ls
qt_packtpub_app.cpp window.cpp window.h
$ qmake -project "QT += widgets"
$ qmake
$ make
$ file qt_packtpub_app
qt_packtpub_app: ELF 32-bit LSB executable, ARM, EABI5 version 1 (SYSV),
dynamically linked, interpreter /lib/ld-linux-armhf.so.3, for GNU/Linux
2.6.32, BuildID[sha1]=4fa5ba7143d8e7fd240da45a9143e9d285371d80, not
stripped
```

Once we have our application ready, we need to generate an image with Qt support for the target that we can use when testing our new application. We will use `rpi-basic-image` as a base, with some additions on top of it. In order to run our Qt application on the target, we need to add a set of packages. For this purpose, a predefined group of packages called `packagegroup-qt5-toolchain-target` can be used. Of course, it's possible to manually point out required Qt5 packages in order to reduce footprint, for example. But in this example, we will keep it simple and ensure that everything we need is included. As stated earlier in the chapter, EGLFS works without any need for a window system, so we can remove X11 and Wayland support to reduce the footprint of the image. All these operations can be specified in `local.conf`:

```
$ echo "IMAGE_INSTALL_append_pn-rpi-basic-image = " packagegroup-qt5-
toolchain-target qt5-opengles2-test"" >> conf/local.conf
$ echo "DISTRO_FEATURES_remove = "x11 wayland"" >> conf/local.conf
```

When the project is configured, we can build the basic image:

```
$ bitbake rpi-basic-image
```

Remember to add the device tree needed for the Raspberry Pi 7 touchscreen, as described earlier in the chapter:

```
$ echo "dtoverlay=rpi-ft5406" >> /path/to/sdcard/boot/config.txt
```

Transfer the newly built application to the target and run it:

```
$ /path/to/qt_packtpub_app -platform eglfs
```

The qt_packpub_app application running on the Raspberry Pi 7 touchscreen

If you were observant during the earlier steps, you would also have seen that we added a package named `qt5-opengles2-test` to our image. This package will produce an OpenGL-based Qt application, which we can use to demonstrate multi-touch actions on our touchscreen:

```
$ qt5-opengles2-test -platform eglfs
```

# Summary

In this chapter we gained some basic knowledge about the Linux kernel and its release strategy and the differences between the mainline kernel and the official Raspberry Pi Linux kernel. We also learned how to configure and compile the Linux kernel using a cross compiler. When changing the `defconfig` file within meta-raspberrypi, the kernel recipe requires some special treatment as compared to the normal Yocto Project procedure. This chapter demonstrated two examples of how this can be done. Later, we also went through some basic kernel configuration required for setting up two different touchscreens; this also included some basic understanding about device trees and how to configure the Raspberry Pi using 'them.

The chapter also covered some examples of how to run a Yocto-based image with a windowing system on the Raspberry Pi, using two different touchscreens: the Raspberry Pi 7 touchscreen and PiTFT 2.8 resistive touchscreen. In the last section of the chapter, we learned about how to run Qt applications built against an SDK generated using the Yocto Project, using a Raspberry Pi and the Raspberry Pi 7 touchscreen.

In the next chapter, we will learn how to contribute to the meta-raspberrypi project.

# 11
# Contributing to the Raspberry Pi BSP Layer

In this chapter, we will learn how to contribute a custom tool to the meta-raspberrypi layer. Common terms associated with the area, such as "open source", "community", and "upstream", will be explained. We will also learn the basics of Git, together with some more advanced Git commands, that can be used together with the sendmail tool.

## Open source

**Open source** can be described as source code available to the general public. Open source software can be read, modified, and redistributed by anyone. This means that developers can use the original code in their own projects without paying any license fee to the owner of the code. Successful open source projects are often built as a community of developers that collaborates and ensures that the open source projects are moving in the intended direction.

The Linux kernel and OpenStack are two of the most famous open source projects. The Yocto Project and it's subprojects are other examples of large open source projects, especially within the embedded world.

Open source communities usually consist of at least one **maintainer**. A maintainer is a person responsible for integrating patches into the project and building the source code. In the integration part, the maintainer often has an important role of either reviewing the patches sent up by developers in the community or making sure it's done by someone else with the right knowledge. In large open source projects such as the Linux kernel, a large number of maintainers exists for different subparts of the kernel. They also appoint a maintainer for each release of the software, who is responsible to maintain the release by, for example, ensuring that important bug fixes are backported.

# Contributing to open source projects

Open source projects are heavily dependent on what people give back to the project, for example, submitting error reports if they find faults in the software or helping the project with solving bugs or developing new features. The community behind an open source project is often limited and doesn't have the resources to do everything by itself. Large projects such as the Linux kernel, OpenStack, and the Yocto Project have large companies behind them, allocating resources for helping out with those projects. The reason for this is obvious: the companies are using the project in commercial products and it's in their interest to make sure that the product has good progress. Many companies also use their own version of the project and want to contribute features and bug fixes in order to decrease the integration cost.

When working with open source, the term **upstream** is used from time to time. **Upstream** could basically be summarized as the original source. The phrase "merge upstream" means that the patch in question should be integrated in the original source code of the project.

# Exploring Git

Git is the version control system used within the Yocto Project, including the Raspberry Pi BSP layer (meta-raspberrypi). Therefore, Git is a central part that you need to master before considering contributing to the Yocto Project and its subprojects.

# What is Git?

**Git** is a distributed version control system that has been around since 2005 and is designed to handle projects with speed and efficiency, regardless of size. It was originally created to handle the source code of the Linux kernel. Git is free and open source and can be used by anyone without any need to pay licensing fees. The design of Git is highly suited to the manner of working used within open source projects. Besides the possibility of using distributed development, it has an easy logging mechanism to record who did what, cryptographic authentication of history, and an easy way to create branches, among other things.

One of the fundamental differences between many other distributed version control systems (VCS, subversion, Bazaar, and so on) is how Git stores information. In Git, the data can be seen as a snapshot of a miniature filesystem. When saving the state of your project, a snapshot is taken of that state and a reference is saved.

The basic Git workflow goes something like this:

- You modify files in your working directory
- You stage the files, adding snapshots of them to your staging area
- You perform a commit, which takes the files as they are in the staging area and stores that snapshot permanently to your Git directory"

For more information, visit
`https://git-scm.com/book/en/v2/Getting-Started-Git-Basics`
.

# Working with Git

A project in Git is called a repository. Most of the work can be done locally by cloning the main repository to your preferred working directory. This is one of the reasons why Git is often considered very fast, when compared with other version control systems that need network access for many operations.

Let's go through some basic examples, which will teach you how to:

- Import an existing project to a Git repository
- Create your first commit
- Convert to a shared repository
- Clone a local version of the shared repository
- Create a work branch
- Push a commit to your shared repository
- Update the cloned repository with the latest changes

When importing an existing project into a new Git repository, we must first initialize an empty Git repository. This can easily be done within the existing source tree of our project:

```
$ tar -zxf my_packt_project_ch_11_01.tar.gz
$ cd  my_packt_project
$ git init
Initialized empty Git repository in  /path/to/repo/my_packt_project/.git/
```

When initializing a new Git repository, a new directory, `.git`, is created. This directory contains all Git-related information about your new repository. Among others things, it contains the main Git configuration file, `config`, which contains the Git settings for your project. Another frequently used file within this directory is `HEAD`, which contains a reference to your current branch.

After the empty Git repository has been created, we can continue with adding all the content of our project to the new repository. A useful command to obtain the current status of your branch and repository is `git status`. When Git isn't aware of a file, it will show up under **Untracked files**, as shown here:

```
$  git status
On branch master
Initial commit
Untracked files:
(use "git add <file>..." to include in what will be committed)
Makefile
README
my_packt_project.c
nothing added to commit but untracked files present (use "git add" to
track)
```

We can add all files and/or changes with a single command, but be aware that it will add build output as well. So, when using `git add --all`, make sure that you have removed unwanted files first. Then, we can use `git status` again to check whether all the expected files are listed:

```
$  git add --all
$  git status
On branch master
Initial commit
Changes to be committed:
(use "git rm --cached <file>..." to unstage)
new file:   Makefile
new file:   README
new file:   my_packt_project.c
```

Before we can submit our changes and create our first commit, we need to set up some basic Git configurations. At the minimum, Git requires you to set up your name and e-mail:

```
$ git config user.email "your_email@packtpub.com"
$ git config user.name "Forename Surname"
```

If you want to set up a global e-mail and name for all your Git repositories, you can specify the `--global` option, like this:

```
$ git config --global user.email "your_email@packtpub.com"
$ git config --global user.name "Forename Surname"
```

To verify the settings, type this:

```
$ git config user.email
your_email@packtpub.com
$ git config user.name
Forename Surname
```

> Global Git configurations are stored in `/home/$USER/.gitconfig` and local ones are stored in `/path/to/git/repository/.git/config`. By default, changes in the local repositories' Git configuration will override changes in your global Git configuration.

When committing a change in Git, the `git commit` command is used. It records changes to the repository and thereby makes it possible to track the commit using the unique SHA-1 hash generated for the commit. An historical overview of a branch can be seen by typing `git log [branch]`.

```
$ git commit -m "My initial commit"
[master (root-commit) f01bdf2] My initial commit
3 files changed, 11 insertions(+)
create mode 100644 Makefile
create mode 100644 README
create mode 100644 my_packt_project.c
$ git log
commit f01bdf29a2c9df1c2417542c5531f90e04c9773a
Author: Forename Surname <you_email@packtpub.com>
Date:   Sun Jan 1 00:00:00 2016 +0100
My initial commit
```

When multiple developers work on the same project, each user uses their own local clone of the repository. Git will by default reject changes pushed to a repository that isn't a `bare` repository. We will now go through a simple example that will:

- Convert our repository to a shared repository
- Clone the shared repository

A shared repository is normally stored on a server and the repository must be created as a bare Git repository. This is done by using the `--bare` flag when initializing the Git repository or while cloning. Since we worked with a non-shared repository in our earlier examples, we will convert it to a shared repository using `git clone --bare`, and we can then remove our old repository and continue working with clones of the bare repository instead.

```
$ cd /path/to/my/workdir
$ git clone --bare /path/to/my_packt_project my_packt_project.git
$ rm -rf /path/to/my_packt_project
```

 A bare repository is basically a repository that doesn't contain a working directory. This will prevent developers from making changes to the repository. According to naming conventions, a bare Git repository should be named `name_of_my_repo.git`.

We now have a bare repository that can be used by a collaboration of developers. Next, we continue with cloning a local copy of the bare repository, which we can use when developing our new features. By default, you will be in a branch called master when cloning a repository. It's possible to do all our work in the master branch; since this is only a local clone, we will not destroy anything for other developers. But it's strongly recommended to create a **working branch** and make all your changes in that branch instead. This way, the master branch is always in a stable and known state. When you are an advanced Git user, you might work on several features in parallel and also might want to integrate new features that other developers have worked on through the master branch. In other words, it's a good habit to create separate branches for all your features.

```
$ git clone /path/to/my_packt_project.git
Cloning into 'my_packt_project'
$ cd my_pack_project
```

Next, we will create a new branch called my_new_feature, move it, and develop a tiny new feature for the project. It's possible to use git branch to list all available local branches; if you add the -a flag when listing branches, all remote branches will be listed as well.

> A remote branch is a branch that exists in a shared repository that has been cloned from. The asterisk (*) helps the user locate the current branch.

```
$ git branch
* master
$ git branch my_new_feature
$ git checkout my_new_feature
Switched to branch 'my_new_feature'
$ git branch
master
* my_new_feature
$ git branch -a
master
* my_new_feature
remotes/origin/HEAD -> origin/master
remotes/origin/master
```

We are now in our new branch and it's time to make some modifications. In this example, we will add a new target, `clean`, to our makefile. Remember to use `git add` in order to add your changes to the index before committing them. Use `git diff` before adding the file if you want to list your changes.

 If you have already added a file using `git add`, you can check your changes before committing them by using `git diff --cached`.

```
$ vim Makefile
$ git diff
diff --git a/Makefile b/Makefile
index c6466e0..d986116 100644
--- a/Makefile
+++ b/Makefile
@@ -1,2 +1,5 @@
all:
$(CC) my_packt_project.c -o my_packt_project
+
+clean:
+rm -f my_packt_project
$ git add Makefile
$ git commit -m "Makefile: Add a new target"
[my_new_feature 7c3d896] Makefile: Add a new target
1 file changed, 3 insertions(+)
```

The last step for us is to send our new change to the shared repository, update our **localmaster** with the new changes, and then remove our feature branch, since it will no longer be required. When pushing a change to our shared repository, we can use the predefined **remote origin**; by default, the origin is set to point to the repository we cloned from. When pushing a change, we need to specify which revision we will send and to which branch. In most situations, we will want to send the entire branch; if so, we can use `HEAD` to obtain all changes from the current branch, like this:

```
$ git push origin HEAD:master
Counting objects: 5, done.
Delta compression using up to 4 threads.
Compressing objects: 100% (3/3), done.
Writing objects: 100% (3/3), 383 bytes | 0 bytes/s, done.
Total 3 (delta 0), reused 0 (delta 0)
To /path/to/my_packt_project.git
f01bdf2..7c3d896  HEAD -> master
$ git checkout master
Switched to branch 'master'
Your branch is behind 'origin/master' by 1 commit, and can be fast-
forwarded.
(use "git pull" to update your local branch)
$ git pull
Updating f01bdf2..7c3d896
Fast-forward
Makefile | 3 +++
1 file changed, 3 insertions(+)
$ git branch -d my_new_feature
Deleted branch my_new_feature (was 7c3d896).
```

If you want to learn more about the basics of Git, visit
https://git-scm.com/doc.

# Contributing to the Yocto Project

Many open source projects, including the Yocto Project, use mailing lists. These lists are mainly used for discussions about the project and public review of patches sent up by the people contributing to the project.

Since the Yocto Project is an umbrella project for a large set of projects, one mailing list isn't enough. For example, there are separate lists for BitBake, OpenEmbedded-Core, and Yocto, where the Yocto includes different external layers, such as meta-raspberrypi and meta-qt5. When sending e-mail to a list used by more then one project, a prefix is required if the mail is intended for a specific subproject (the syntax for the prefix is `[layername] subject`). The following screenshot illustrates an example of sending a series of patches to meta-raspberrypi:

- [yocto] [meta-raspberrypi][PATCH 0/5] Various upgrade/fixes from Technux  *Petter Mabäcker*
  - [yocto] [meta-raspberrypi][PATCH 1/5] .gitignore: Ignore .swp files  *Petter Mabäcker*
  - [yocto] [meta-raspberrypi][PATCH 2/5] linux-raspberrypi: Update 4.1 recipe to 4.1.15  *Petter Mabäcker*
  - [yocto] [meta-raspberrypi][PATCH 3/5] rpi-config: I2C support  *Petter Mabäcker*
  - [yocto] [meta-raspberrypi][PATCH 4/5] pitft: Add basic support for PiTFT  *Petter Mabäcker*
    - [yocto] [meta-raspberrypi][PATCH 4/5] pitft: Add basic support for PiTFT  *Khem Raj*
      - [yocto] [meta-raspberrypi][PATCH 4/5] pitft: Add basic support for PiTFT  *Andrei Gherzan*
      - [yocto] [meta-raspberrypi][PATCH 4/5] pitft: Add basic support for PiTFT  *Petter Mabäcker*
      - [yocto] [meta-raspberrypi][PATCH 4/5] pitft: Add basic support for PiTFT  *Khem Raj*
      - [yocto] [meta-raspberrypi][PATCH 4/5] pitft: Add basic support for PiTFT  *Petter Mabäcker*
  - [yocto] [meta-raspberrypi][PATCH 5/5] pitft: Add PiTFT22 support  *Petter Mabäcker*
  - [yocto] [meta-raspberrypi][PATCH 0/5] Various upgrade/fixes from Technux  *Petter Mabäcker*

The mailing lists can be easily tracked by subscribing to a specific mailing list or by reading the archives.

All Yocto Project mailing lists can be found at
`https://www.yoctoproject.org/tools-resources/community/mailing-lists`

# Contributing to meta-raspberrypi

If you have prepared a fix or feature for meta-raspberrypithat you want to share with the community, there are a number of things you need to be aware of.

The current maintainer of meta-raspberrypi is Andrei Gherzan. He has the final word about a patch and will integrate the patch into the meta-raspberrypi main layer. Since the maintainers are quite busy, it's important that you test your patch carefully before sending it upstream. The most important thing for a contributor, regardless of the project, is to build up its reputation by sending well-tested patches that follow the requested guidelines. This will significantly increase the chances of getting your patch integrated into the project.

Some overall "rules" exist for contributing to meta-raspberrypi:

- Patches related to meta-raspberrypi should always be sent to
  yocto@yoctoproject.org.
- Prefix your emails with "**[meta-raspberrypi]**"
- Follow the OpenEmbedded patch guidelines
- Follow the meta-raspberrypi readme instructions

An extended explanation of this set of rules, together with examples, will be described later in this chapter.

# Setting up your Git repository

Before you can send anything upstream, you need set up some basic things. First, you should set up your name and e-mail for your meta-raspberrypi Git repository, as described in earlier parts of this chapter:

```
$ cd meta-raspberrypi
$ git config user.email "your_email@packtpub.com"
$ git config user.name "Forename Surname"
```

Next, you should set up git send-email in order to use Git to send your patches through your SMTP server. This is often required by the maintainers in order to ensure that the format of the patch is correct and it can be easily integrated. You need to manually configure the server parameters-refer to your e-mail provider's documentation or contact support in order to find the right parameters.

In addition to Git, you also need to install send-email, which is the software Git uses under the hood for git send-email. The send-email package is available on most distributions, but the name might differ. Here is how to set it up on Ubuntu and Fedora:

- **Ubuntu**: $ sudo apt-get install sendemail
- **Fedora**: $ sudo yum install sendmail

Here is an example of how to configure `sendemail`:

```
$ cd meta-raspberrypi
$ git config sendemail.smtpencryption tls
$ git config sendemail.smtpserver smtp.packtpub.com
$ git config sendemail.smtpuser your_email@packtpub.com
$ git config sendemail.smtpserverport 587
```

# Creating your commit

Now, you are ready to make your modifications. In this subsection, we will go through each step from implementing your changes to creating a commit that follows the patch guidelines for meta-raspberrypi.

It is common sense to create your changes in a working branch (not the master branch). In our example, we will set up a branch that tracks the master branch:

```
$ cd meta-raspberrypi
$ git checkout -b my_work_branch -t origin/master
```

Now, using your favorite editor, edit the files you want to change. When you are done with your modifications, you need to add the changed files to the Git index; otherwise, Git will not add your changes to the upcoming commit:

```
$ git add <files changed>
```

Now it's time to create a commit message by following the guidelines in the meta-raspberrypi' readme and the openembedded guidelines. Here are the most important parts of the guidelines:

## New Development

A minimal patch or commit message would be of the format:

```
Short log / Statement of what needed to be changed.

(Optional pointers to external resources, such as defect tracking)

The intent of your change.

(Optional, if it's not clear from above) how your change resolves the
issues in the first part.

Tag line(s) at the end.
```

For example:

```
foobar: Adjusted the foo setting in bar

When using foobar on systems with less than a gigabyte of RAM common
usage patterns often result in an Out-of-memory condition causing
slowdowns and unexpected application termination.

Low-memory systems should continue to function without running into
memory-starvation conditions with minimal cost to systems with more
available memory.  High-memory systems will be less able to use the
full extent of the system, a dynamically tunable option may be best,
long-term.

The foo setting in bar was decreased from X to X-50% in order to
ensure we don't exhaust all system memory with foobar threads.

Signed-off-by: Joe Developer <joe.developer@example.com>
```

The complete OpenEmbedded guidelines can be found at
http://www.openembedded.org/wiki/Commit_Patch_Message_Gui
delines.

When creating the commit, remember to sign off on it (using -s). The signoff is a one-liner that is added by default to the end of the commit message. The original purpose of the signoff is as follows, according to the Linux kernel documentation:

> *"To improve tracking of who did what, especially with patches that can percolate to their final resting place in the kernel through several layers of maintainers, we've introduced a "sign-off" procedure on patches that are being emailed around. The sign-off is a simple line at the end of the explanation for the patch, which certifies that you wrote it or otherwise have the right to pass it on as an open-source patch."*

Here is how you use it:

```
$ git commit -s
Write your commit message
```

# Sending changes to the community

The maintainers of a project want to focus on the design of your patches and often assume that patches sent to the list are functional. Therefore, it's important to ensure that you have verified that the patch has been built and tested for relevant images supported by meta-raspberrypi.

When your patch meets your expectations and has passed all tests, it's time to send it to the community. First, we need to generate the patch. When generating a patch, we should follow the recommendations from the readme in meta-raspberrypi. If you have more than one commit, one patch for each commit will be generated. A cover letter will also be generated, and it will always be named 0000-cover-letter.patch. The cover letter is optional but strongly recommended when creating more then one patch in the same series.

```
$ git format-patch --cover-letter --subject-prefix='meta-
raspberrypi][PATCH' origin
```

 Remove "–cover-letter" if you only have one patch or don't feel the need for it.

If you decide to generate a cover letter, you can open it with your preferred editor. Search for the lines *** SUBJECT HERE *** and *** BLURB HERE *** and replace them with appropriate information about your patches.

Time for the final step: sending the patches up to the mailing list!

```
$ git send-email --to yocto@yoctoproject.org <generated patches>
```

# Follow-up

By now, your patches should have reached the mailing list, and you can sit back for a while and wait for feedback. If you receive feedback from the mailing list, you are expected to reply with an answer saying that you will perform the requested changes or, if you disagree, reply with an 'appropriate reason for why you don't.

Don't be scared if you receive feedback; this is normal. In fact, many of the changes sent to the mailing list will need updates before they are ready to be integrated into the main layer.

When sending an update of your patch to the mailing list, it's important that you specify the version number of your patch series. This can easily be done by slightly modifying the line used when you generated the patch in the first place (pay attention to the new subject prefix):

```
$ git format-patch --cover-letter --subject-prefix='meta-raspberrypi][PATCH
v2' origin
```

> Remove "–cover-letter" if you only have one patch or don't feel the need for it.

If your patch needs yet another update, just increment the version number and try again. When your patch has reached the meta-raspberrypi layer, you are done and can continue working with some other feature that interests you.

# Practical example – sending a custom tool upstream

In this section, we will go through a practical example of integrating a custom tool into meta-raspberrypi. The tool we have chosen is **con2fbmap**, a command-line tool for setting and showing mappings between framebuffer TFT devices (such as PiTFT displays) and consoles.

First of all, we need to identify where in the layer structure we should place our new recipe. In some situations, we can guess the location by reading the name of the package. One example of this is the `omxplayer` recipe. It's quite easy to figure out that it should be placed among the multimedia recipes (recipes-multimedia). If we cannot use the package name to find a location, we can check whether a similar tool exists. For our example, meta-oe (the openembedded base layer) contains a somewhat similar tool called **fbset**. It's a tool for modifying framebuffer devices. If we locate the **fbset** recipe, we can see that it's placed within recipes-support, and we should probably place our package in that directory as well.

You can find the fbset tool at
`https://github.com/openembedded/meta-openembedded/tree/master/meta-oe/recipes-support/fbset`, as shown here:

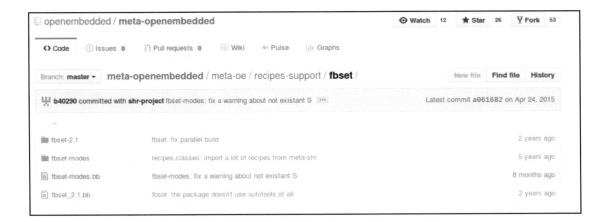

When creating a new recipe, you can either use the tools described in `Chapter 7`, Deploying a Custom Layer on the Raspberry Pi or create it from scratch. In this example, we will create it from scratch. The first thing we need to know is which kind of source (such as .tar.gz or Git) the tool has. In this case, the original source is Git, and we can create a basic recipe for `con2fbmap`, as follows:

```
$ cd meta-raspberrypi
$ mkdir -p recipes-support/con2fbmap
$ cd recipes-support/con2fbmap
$ touch con2fbmap_git.bb
```

Use your favorite editor and create the content for the BitBake file (.bb). In this book, we have chosen to use a "known state" and set SRCREV to **f57bf6d28910ba665efab8a65085ba6d4c6162a5**. Other information in the BitBake file, such as `LIC_FILES_CHKSUM`, will be based upon this particular SRCREV value. The complete `con2fbmap_git.bb` file looks like this:

```
SUMMARY = "Utility for swapping an fbtft-based device"
DESCRIPTION = "Simple utility for swapping an fbtft-based device as \
the console"
LICENSE = "GPLv3"
LIC_FILES_CHKSUM = "file://COPYING;md5=d32239bcb673463ab874e80d47fae504"
SECTION = "console/utils"
Inherit autotools
SRC_URI =
"git://gitlab.com/pibox/con2fbmap.git;branch=master;protocol=https"
SRCREV = "f57bf6d28910ba665efab8a65085ba6d4c6162a5"
S = "${WORKDIR}/git"
```

Remember to build and verify the new recipe. When you are satisfied with your changes, you can go ahead and create your new Git commit. Make sure that you follow the guidelines when writing your commit message.

```
$ git add con2fbmap_git.bb
$ git commit -s
con2fbmap: Add new recipe
Currently there is no easy way to manually switch between
framebuffer devices and console during run-time.
This tool can be used when the system is up and running, to
set and show mapping between framebuffer tft devices
(such as pitft displays) and the consoles.
Signed-off-by: Petter Mabäcker <petter@technux.se>
# Please enter the commit message for your changes. Lines starting
# with '#' will be ignored, and an empty message aborts the commit.
```

Once you are satisfied with your commit message, it's time to generate the patches. Since all changes in this example will fit into one Git commit, we can skip the `--cover-letter` flag.

```
$ git format-patch --subject-prefix='meta-raspberrypi][PATCH' origin
0001-con2fbmap-Add-new-recipe.patch
```

When the tool has been built and carefully tested on the target, we can send it to the mailing list:

```
git send-email --to yocto@yoctoproject.org 0001-con2fbmap-Add-new-recipe.patch
```

You have now learned how to contribute to the main layer. A good piece of advice is to be patient when working with an open source community. Depending on which state the project is in, maintainers and other people responsible for integrating changes might be busy, and sometimes, it takes time until they respond to your patch. If you haven't heard anything in a while, don't be afraid to send a friendly reminder to people on the list to look at your patch.

# Summary

In this chapter, we had an overview of open source software and how to work with open source projects. Some of the major benefits of contributing to open source, such as decreasing integration cost for your product, were highlighted. We also learned the basics of Git and some more advanced Git commands, which can be used in combination with the sendmail binary, in order to send patches to an open source community. Finally, we took a walkthrough of a real-world example, by learning how to integrate the custom tool con2fbmap into meta-raspberrypi and send it for review to the Yocto Project community.

In the next chapter, we will summarize all that we have learned through this book by creating a home automation project.

# 12
# Home Automation Project - Booting a Custom Image

The Internet of Things is a very hot subject today. Using automation within the home to ease daily tasks has gained more importance than ever. The Raspberry Pi, due to its size, price, and the possibilities to easily connect it to other electronics equipment, is a very good choice for making small home automation projects. This chapter will guide you through a small home automation project that will let you set up a remote lighting control system using the Raspberry Pi and then control it remotely with the help of a smartphone. The project will require skills learned in earlier chapters, so this chapter will also act as a summary of all you have learned throughout the book.

The chapter will start with an introduction to our home automation project and the material that is required for it. Then, it will go into the integration of Yocto with our project. This section of the chapter will explain how to set up up the image used by the Raspberry Pi: it will cover things such as creating a new layer containing our new image recipe and adding/modifying packages required for our project. The chapter will end with a section that puts everything together. It will explain how all the physical parts should be connected and how to remote control the device using different devices, such as a smartphone or another Raspberry Pi with touchscreen.

## Home automation using a Raspberry Pi

Our home automation project will loosely continue from the "light an LED" example in Chapter 5, Creating, Developing, and Deploying on the Raspberry Pi. It will adapt and evolve that project to create one where the end user can wirelessly light a lamp using a smartphone (or some other device with a web browser).

As illustrated in the following diagram, the idea is to connect a one-channel relay module to the Raspberry Pi, using the GPIO pins. Then, we connect a lamp and an external power source to the relay module, creating a circuit. When everything has been connected, it will be possible to control the relay module (on/off) using GPIO connections from the Raspberry Pi.

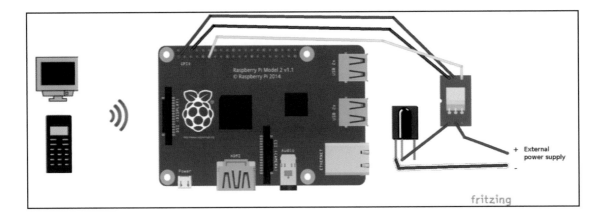

A home automation project that enables remote lighting

# Material required for the project

You will need the following material for the project:

- A Raspberry Pi (any model will do)

    The Raspberry Pi Zero requires that you either solder in a GPIO header or solder the wires directly to the GPIO pads

- Jumper cables (three are required)
- A one-channel 5V relay module
- A lamp (preferably a lamp you don't mind splitting and cutting the cable of)
- An external power supply (preferably 12V)

 WARNING: This project requires basic knowledge of electrical circuits. We strongly discourage using high-voltage power if you don't have the knowledge or experience.

# Setting up the base for the project

First, we should set up the base for our Yocto Project implementation. Most of the techniques used in this section have been covered throughout the book, so they will not be explained in detail. In this part of the chapter, we perform the basic setup for our Yocto Project implementation, which will be used for the home automation project.

# Creating a new layer

We will begin by creating a new layer. The new layer will act as the base of our home automation project. For now, it will only contain our image recipe, but we will add more content to the layer throughout the chapter until we have all the parts needed for our server. Just as described in Chapter 7, *Deploying a Custom Layer on the Raspberry Pi*, we will use **yocto-layer** to help us set up the structure of the layer. We need to set a high priority to ensure that content from this layer is prioritized over, for example, content in meta-raspberrypi, like so:

```
$ /path/to/poky/scripts/yocto-layer create packt-iot
Please enter the layer priority you'd like to use for the layer: [default:
6] 10
Would you like to have an example recipe created? (y/n) [default: n]
Would you like to have an example bbappend file created? (y/n) [default: n]
New layer created in meta-packt-iot.
Don't forget to add it to your BBLAYERS (for details see meta-packt-
iot/README).
```

# Customizing the image recipe

In this subsection, we will improve upon the usage of a customized image recipe, which we learned in Chapter 7, *Deploying a Custom Layer on the Raspberry Pi.*.

Start by creating your image recipe file:

```
$ cd meta-packt-iot
$ mkdir -p recipes-core/images/
$ touch recipes-core/images/packt-iot-image.bb
```

Next, we will set up the basic content of the image; take a look at the following code snippet. This image recipe will be growing during the entire chapter until we finally have a complete image that fits our purpose. The image will be based on **rpi-basic-image**.

```
$ cat recipes-core/images/packt-iot-image.bb
# Base this image on rpi-basic-image
include recipes-core/images/rpi-basic-image.bb
SPLASH = "psplash-raspberrypi"
IMAGE_FEATURES += "ssh-server-dropbear splash"
IMAGE_INSTALL_append = " rpi-gpio"
```

When working with image recipes, two commands called ROOTFS_PREPROCESS_COMMAND and ROOTFS_POSTPROCESS_COMMAND exist. They can be used as the last resort to, for example, add, remove, or modify content in the root filesystem. The two methods can be used either just *before* the root filesystem is created using the PREPROCESS variant or *after* the root filesystem has been created using the POSTPROCESS method. They are used by specifying a list of functions to the variable. The functions can use ${IMAGE_ROOTFS} to, in a generic way, find out the path to the filesystem. For this project, we will use this method to add a function to ROOTFS_POSTPROCESS_COMMAND that will create a release file for our image. Add the following content last in packt-iot-image.bb:

```
ROOTFS_POSTPROCESS_COMMAND += " create_release_file ; "
create_release_file() {
IMAGE_REL_FILE="${IMAGE_ROOTFS}${sysconfdir}/packt-iot-release"
    echo "packt-iot release version 1.0" > ${IMAGE_REL_FILE}
    echo "Image: ${IMAGE_NAME}" >> ${IMAGE_REL_FILE}
    echo "Build date: ${DATETIME}" >> ${IMAGE_REL_FILE}
    chmod 0444 ${IMAGE_REL_FILE}
}
```

Take careful notice of the whitespace in the create_release_file; part of the ROOTFS_POSTPROCESS_COMMAND declaration.

# Building and booting the image

We now have a new external layer containing a basic image recipe. Until now, we haven't done any testing of the layer. It is always a good idea to perform regular tests of your changes during development. We will perform an early test of our layer. In order to do this, we will create a new project, set up some mandatory and good-to-have configurations in local.conf, and add external layers to bblayers.conf. This project will then be used throughout the chapter.

```
$ source /path/to/poky/oe-init-build-env packt_project_chapter12
```

Add the `meta-raspberrypi` and `meta-oe` external layers, together with our new `meta-packt-iot` layer, to `bblayers.conf`:

```
BBLAYERS ?= " \
  /path/to/poky/meta \
  /path/to/poky/meta-poky \
  /path/to/poky/meta-yocto-bsp \
  /path/to/meta-raspberrypi \
  /path/to/meta-openembedded/meta-oe \
  /path/to/meta-packt-iot \
  "
```

Decide which machine to use and add it to `local.conf`. In this example, we will use `raspberrypi2`:

```
$ echo "MACHINE = "raspberrypi2"" >> conf/local.conf
```

We will next enable a local **package revision** (**PR**) server in our project. The PR server will automatically bump the PR of a package if a change is detected. This will be done without a need for the end user, to manually update the PR number in the recipe file. This feature is very handy during, for example, the development of new recipes:

```
$ echo "PRSERV_HOST = "localhost:0"" >> conf/local.conf
```

A project in BitBake can consume a lot of disk space. There exist a number of methods that can be used to reduce both the amount of disk space used by a project and its overall build time.

The first method is to use `rm_work`. This feature will make sure that BitBake performs a full cleanup of packages that have been built. By default, all built packages will have source and artifacts saved in package-specific locations, under `./tmp/work` in the project. These will be wiped when the following class is inherited for the project:

```
$ echo "INHERIT += "rm_work"" >> conf/local.conf
```

However, it might be good to exclude packages that are frequently used during development, especially if it takes a long time unpack them. To achieve this, `RM_WORK_EXCLUDE` can be used.

The build time for a project is often quite long, especially the first time, since BitBake needs to fetch all source and build packages from scratch. But after the first build is done, you can use a number of methods to speed up subsequent builds. These methods can also be used in other Yocto projects with a similar setup to decrease the build time and amount of disk space needed. The first method is to use a shared state (sstate) . By default, the sstate cache is located within the project. But by using the SSTATE_DIR variable in local.conf, the shared state can be located outside of a project and be used by other projects as well. The same goes for the next method, which is specifying the download location for all packages fetched by BitBake during the build. It can also be configured from local.conf using the DL_DIR variable. In this example, we will not use a shared state or a download directory outside of our project. The reason for this is that it isn't recommended when using a local PR server.

At this point, your local.conf file should look something like this:

```
$ tail conf/local.conf
PACKAGECONFIG_append_pn-nativesdk-qemu = " sdl"
#ASSUME_PROVIDED += "libsdl-native"
# CONF_VERSION is increased each time build/conf/ changes incompatibly and
is used to
# track the version of this file when it was generated. This can safely be
ignored if
# this doesn't mean anything to you.
CONF_VERSION = "1"
MACHINE = "raspberrypi2"
PRSERV_HOST = "localhost:0"
INHERIT += "rm_work"
```

When the project has its initial configuration in place, we can build the image created earlier in this chapter:

```
$ bitbake packt-iot-image                                    Parsing
recipes: 100%
|#####################################################################
############################| Time: 00:00:31
Parsing of 895 .bb files complete (0 cached, 895 parsed). 1325 targets, 68
skipped, 0 masked, 0 errors.
NOTE: Resolving any missing task queue dependencies
```

Let's try our new image on the target. In this state, the image should behave similarly to a normal **rpi-basic-image** image. It's always good to not only build our changes but also test them on the target in order to ensure that nothing gets broken along the road. Use the method described in Chapter 2, *Building our First Poky Image for the Raspberry Pi* to copy the image to an SD card (remember to change /dev/sdX to the proper device name):

```
$ sudo dd
if=/path/to/packt_project_chapter12/tmp/deploy/images/raspberrypi2/packt-
iot-image-raspberrypi2.rpi-sdimg of=/dev/sdX bs=1M
```

Next, insert the SD card into the Raspberry Pi and power it on. The image doesn't contain any big changes from rpi-basic-image; still, we can easily see that we are running the correct image. As you might remember, we added a post function in the image recipe, which added a release file. Let's check whether it exists and check the content (log in using root and an empty password):

```
Poky (Yocto Project Reference Distro) 2.0+snapshot-20160229 raspberrypi2
/dev/ttyAMA0
    raspberrypi2 login: root
    root@raspberrypi2:~# ls /etc/*release*
    /etc/packt-iot-release
    root@raspberrypi2:~# cat /etc/packt-iot-release
    packt-iot release version 1.0
    Image: packt-iot-image-raspberrypi2-20160304085812
    Build date: 20160304085812
    root@raspberrypi2:~#
```

# Creating the server side

We now have the base ready and can continue with implementing the project-specific parts. The Raspberry Pi that is connected with the circuit and the lamp will act as a server. It will run a tiny web server that can be reached through a client of your choice using a web browser.

For the server side, we will adapt and evolve the server example used in Chapter 9, Making a Media Hub on the Raspberry Pi, and combine it with an updated version of the gpio-packt recipe from Chapter 5, Creating, Developing, and Deploying on the Raspberry Pi, . To start with, we need to add the meta-packt_rpi layer used in earlier chapters of the book. We have already ensured that our newly created layer has a higher priority then meta-packt_rpi, but let's also add it in a dependency order in bblayers.conf. Here is the complete bblayers.conf file that will be used in this project:

```
# LAYER_CONF_VERSION is increased each time build/conf/bblayers.conf
# changes incompatibly
POKY_BBLAYERS_CONF_VERSION = "1"
BBPATH = "${TOPDIR}"
BBFILES ?= ""
BBLAYERS ?= " \
      /path/to/poky/meta \
      /path/to/poky/meta-poky \
      /path/to/poky/meta-yocto-bsp \
      /path/to/meta-raspberrypi \
      /path/to/meta-openembedded/meta-oe \
      /path/to/meta-packt_rpi \
      /path/to/meta-packt-iot \
      "
BBLAYERS_NON_REMOVABLE ?= " \
      /home/path/to/git/poky/meta \
      /home/path/to/git/poky/meta-yocto \
      "
```

Next, we should make some minor changes to gpio-packt in order to make it more suitable for our project. These changes will be made as a integration patch. The original code uses **GPIO4,** which is one of the pins that are set high by default. We will instead use **GPIO17**, which is one of the pins that defaults to low.

To change the `gpio_example` code to use GPIO17 instead, we can create a new integration patch that changes the behavior only when we apply the `meta-packt-iot` layer. The minor changes required are as follows:

```
--- gpio_example.c.orig 2016-03-10 16:55:04.334832221 +0100
+++ gpio_example.c      2016-03-10 16:54:13.400537071 +0100
@@ -39,7 +39,7 @@
/*===============================================*/
#define       LENGTH          128
#define       SYSFS_GPIO_DIR  "/sys/class/gpio/"
-#define       GPIO_PIN        4
+#define       GPIO_PIN        17
#define       BUFFER_SIZE       255
#define       DEBUG           1
#define       VERSION         1.00
```

The patch can be generated by using the `diff` command. This will result in a difference between the original version of `gpio_example.c` and the updated version.

```
$ diff -Naur gpio_example.c.orig gpio_example.c > use_gpio17.patch
```

Next, we must add the patch to `meta-packt-iot`. Start by creating the structure for appending `gpio_example` in `meta-packt-iot`:

```
./recipes-custom
./recipes-custom/gpio-packt
./recipes-custom/gpio-packt/gpio-packt
./recipes-custom/gpio-packt/gpio-packt/use_gpio17.patch
./recipes-custom/gpio-packt/gpio-packt_0.1.bbappend
```

The content of the `bbappend` will be very small and will only be required to apply the patch:

```
FILESEXTRAPATHS_prepend := "${THISDIR}/${PN}:"
SRC_URI += " \
file://use_gpio17.patch;striplevel=0 \
"
```

Time to start with the web server. We need to make some modifications to our project for the server part as well. Most of the basic setup can be kept as is for the `webserver-packt` recipe. However, the server JavaScript (`server.js`) and the main webpage (`index.html`) need new logic and content. Since the new content is not really suitable to add to the existing code, we will create a new `bbappend` file for the web server and then override the package with new versions of the `index.html` and `server.js` files that are suitable for this specific project. Start by creating a new structure within `meta-packt-iot` that looks like this (`index.html`, `server.js`, and `webserver-packt_0.1.bbappend` can be empty for now):

```
./recipes-custom
./recipes-custom/webserver-packt
./recipes-custom/webserver-packt/webserver-packt_0.1.bbappend
./recipes-custom/webserver-packt/webserver-packt
./recipes-custom/webserver-packt/webserver-packt/index.html
./recipes-custom/webserver-packt/webserver-packt/server.js
```

When the new structure is in place, we can start with adding content to the `bbappend` file:

```
DESCRIPTION = "Remote lighting control"
FILESEXTRAPATHS_prepend := "${THISDIR}/${PN}:"
SRC_URI += " \
    file://server.js \
    file://index.html \
    "
do_install_append() {
    install -d ${D}${datadir}/server-packt/server
    install -m 0755 ${WORKDIR}/index.html ${D}${datadir}/server-
packt/server/public/index.html
    install -m 0755 ${WORKDIR}/server.js ${D}${datadir}/server-
packt/server/server.js
}
```

The logic in `webserver-packt_0.1.bbappend` is quite simple. It appends the `SRC_URI` variable with our new versions of `index.html` and `server.js` and then overrides the old files in the install stage.

Let's take a deeper look at the code modifications needed for our project. Just like in the media hub example in Chapter 9, Making a Media Hub on the Raspberry Pi we will continue to serve an HTML file that will act as the client. We will also continue to listen on the same port (3344) to avoid confusion. The functional logic in the server code lies within the io.on() {...} function. Here, we will receive a message from the client (index.html) and execute it on the server. In our example, the command to execute is either gpio_example --led=1 or gpio_example --led=0, which will cause the light to turn on and off, respectively. The complete code for server.js looks like this:

```
var express = require('express')
    , app = express()
    , server = require('http').createServer(app)
    , path = require('path'),
    fs = require('fs'),
    sys = require('util'),
    exec = require('child_process').exec,
    child, child1;
http://192.168.1.13:3344/light.html
io = require('socket.io').listen(server),
                io.set('log level', 1); /* DEBUG MODE */
app.use(express.static(path.join(__dirname, 'public')));
app.get('/', function(req, res) {
    res.sendFile(__dirname + '/public/index.html');
});
io.on('connection', function(socket) {
    socket.on('light', function(msg) {
        child = exec(msg, function (error, stdout, stderr) {
            if (error !== null) {
                console.log('exec error: ' + error);
            }
        });
    });
});

server.listen(3344, function() {
    console.log('listening on *:3344');
});
```

To get the whole picture of the solution, we also need to look at the client, `index.html`. The look and feel of the web page from `Chapter 9`, *Making a Media Hub on the Raspberry Pi* is kept, but the CPU monitoring has been replaced by a green/red button, used to turn the light on or off. Depending on which button is pushed, a socket message using `socket.emit` is used. The message contains the exact Unix command required to turn the light on or off:

```
<body>
<nav class="navbar navbar-inverse navbar-fixed-top" role="navigation">
<div class="container-fluid">
<div class="navbar-header">
<button type="button" class="navbar-toggle collapsed" data-
toggle="collapse" data-target="#bs-example-navbar-collapse-1">
<span class="sr-only">Toggle navigation</span>
<span class="icon-bar"></span>
<span class="icon-bar"></span>
<span class="icon-bar"></span>
</button>
 <ul class="nav navbar-nav">
    <li class="active"> <a href="index.html">HOME</a> </li>
  </ul>
</div>
</div>
</div>
</nav>'
<hr>
<div class="container-fluid">
<div class="well well-lg text-center">
<h1><b>Raspberry-Pi</b><b></b></h1>
<p><b>Remote lighting</b> control</p>
<h4><span class="label label-info"></span></h4>
</div>
<button class="button buttonON" onclick="lighton()">ON </button>
<button class="button buttonOFF" onclick="lightoff()">OFF</button>
<script src="/socket.io/socket.io.js"></script>
<script>
    var socket = io.connect('http://'+ location.host);
    function lighton()
    {
        socket.emit('light', 'gpio_example --led=1');
        return false;
    }
    function lightoff()
    {
        socket.emit('light', 'gpio_example --led=0');
        return false;
    }
}
```

```
</script>
</body>
```

If you look at `index.html` in a web browser, it should look like this:

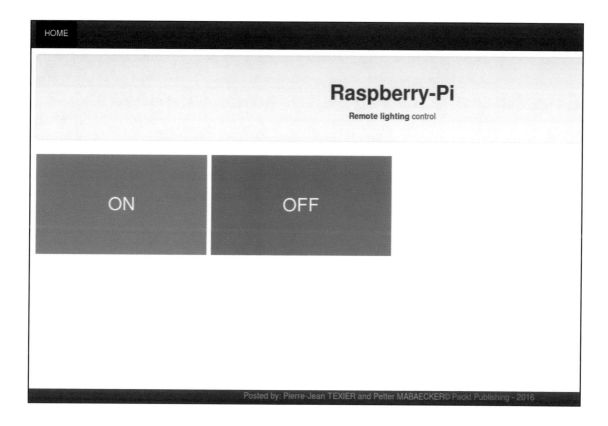

The look of the client (index.html) when displayed in a web browser

Lastly, we must not forget to add `gpio-packt` and `webserver-packt` to our image:

```
$ cat recipes-core/images/packt-iot-image.bb
# Base this image on rpi-basic-image
include recipes-core/images/rpi-basic-image.bb
SPLASH = "psplash-raspberrypi"
IMAGE_FEATURES += "ssh-server-dropbear splash"
IMAGE_INSTALL_append = " rpi-gpio gpio-packt webserver-packt"
```

# Creating a packet list for your image

One of the reasons you would want to create a customized image is that you often require a different set of packages than those used in existing images. When using the Yocto Project, it's possible to use a sort of package list, to make it easier for the end user to add new packages and to keep the image recipe as simple as possible. This section will guide your through how to use a customized package list using the Yocto Project.

## Setting up a customized package list

First, you need to add a new BitBake file (`.bb`) named `packagegroup-packt-iot.bb`:

```
$ mkdir recipes-core/images/packagegroups
$ touch  packagegroup-packt-iot.bb
```

A typical package list will look something like this:

```
$ cat packagegroup-packt-iot.bb
DESCRIPTION = "Package list for packt-iot-image"
LICENSE = "MIT"
inherit packagegroup
RDEPENDS_${PN} += " \
  pkg1 \
  pkg2 \
  pkg3 \
  "
```

# Start using a customized package list in meta-packt-iot

When our customized package list is in place, we can transfer packages added through `IMAGE_INSTALL`. This will make the package group look like the following:

```
$ cat packagegroup-packt-iot.bb
DESCRIPTION = "Package list for packt-iot-image"
LICENSE = "MIT"
inherit packagegroup
RDEPENDS_${PN} += " \
  rpi-gpio \
  nodejs \
  gpio-packt \
  webserver-packt \
  "
```

Finally, we need to ensure that our new package list is used; for this example, it will be done by replacing the content in `IMAGE_INSTALL` with the package group recipe, like this:

```
# Base this image on rpi-basic-image
include recipes-core/images/rpi-basic-image.bb
SPLASH = "psplash-raspberrypi"
IMAGE_FEATURES += "ssh-server-dropbear splash"
IMAGE_INSTALL_append = " packagegroup-packt-iot"
```

The Yocto Project documentation contains the following information about `IMAGE_INSTALL`:

"Using IMAGE_INSTALL with the += operator from the /conf/local.conf file or from within an image recipe is not recommended as it can cause ordering issues. Since core-image.bbclass sets IMAGE_INSTALL to a default value using the ?= operator, using a += operation against IMAGE_INSTALL will result in unexpected behavior when used in conf/local.conf. Furthermore, the same operation from within an image recipe may or may not succeed depending on the specific situation. In both these cases, the behavior is contrary to how most users expect the += operator to work."

For more details, visit `http://www.yoctoproject.org/docs/current/ref-manual/ref-manual.html#var-IMAGE_INSTALL`.

# Putting it all together

At this point, we have a basic idea about how to build our project, and we also have all the software required for our project. In this section, we will go through a number of iterations until we reach the final goal of using a remote device to control the lamp.

We will do this in three steps:

1. Control the relay using the Raspberry Pi.
2. Control the lamp using the Raspberry Pi.
3. Turn on/off the lamp from a smartphone.

During development, it's inefficient to always boot the Raspberry Pi using, for example, an HDMI connection to a TV that also requires a separate mouse and keyboard to control the Pi. Using HDMI, we will not be able to track the early boot procedure either. For this project, we also want to be able to troubleshoot the Raspberry Pi without the need to place it close to a TV. For our project, we will either use SSH or a serial connection to reduce turnaround time during development.

## Serial and SSH connections to the Raspberry Pi

The first method is to use a serial connection to the Raspberry Pi. The easiest way to achieve this is to use a USB-to-serial cable. Connect the USB to the your host machine. Then, connect the four wire cables to the correct GPIO pins on the Raspberry Pi, as showed in the following figure:

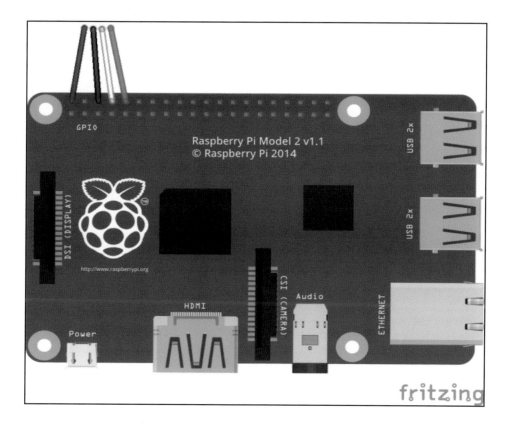

A USB-to-serial cable connected to the Raspberry Pi GPIO header

The following table will give a more detailed explanation of how the GPIO wires should be connected. Also check the GPIO header diagram in `Chapter 8`, *Diving into the Raspberry Pis Peripherals and Yocto Recipes.* to review the purpose of all the pins in the GPIO header.

| Red | 5V |
|---|---|
| Black | GND |
| White | GPIO 14 (TXD) |
| Green | GPIO 15 (RXD) |

Once the physical connection has been set up, we can continue with preparing our host environment. In this example, we will use the `screen` package to set up our console connection.

To set up `screen` on Ubuntu, use this command:

```
$ sudo apt-get install screen
```

Use this one to set it up on Fedora:

```
$ sudo yum install screen
```

Next, we must ensure that we have plugged in the USB cable to our Raspberry Pi (remember that no additional power supply is needed). After that, we can open a terminal window and type the following command, which will connect us to the Raspberry Pi console:

```
$ sudo screen /dev/ttyUSB0 115200
<snip>
[    2.017380] [vc_sm_connected_init]: end - returning 0
[    2.023899] uart-pl011 3f201000.uart: no DMA platform data
[    2.034527] EXT4-fs (mmcblk0p2): INFO: recovery required on readonly
filesystem
[    2.041844] EXT4-fs (mmcblk0p2): write access will be enabled during
recovery
[    2.093584] EXT4-fs (mmcblk0p2): recovery complete
[    2.103945] EXT4-fs (mmcblk0p2): mounted filesystem with ordered data
mode. Opts: (null)
[    2.112154] VFS: Mounted root (ext4 filesystem) readonly on device
179:2.
[    2.122995] devtmpfs: mounted
.
.
.
Starting syslogd/klogd: done
Poky (Yocto Project Reference Distro) 2.0+snapshot-20160229 raspberrypi2
/dev/ttyAMA0
 raspberrypi2 login: [   17.906610] random: nonblocking pool is initialized
Poky (Yocto Project Reference Distro) 2.0+snapshot-20160229 raspberrypi2
/dev/ttyAMA0
raspberrypi2 login:
```

If we have connected a network cable to the Raspberry Pi, we can use this method to grab the IP address of our board:

```
root@raspberrypi2:~# ifconfig eth0 | grep "inet addr"
inet addr:192.168.1.13  Bcast:192.168.1.255  Mask:255.255.255.0
```

The other method to gain quick access to the Raspberry Pi without using any external equipment (such as a mouse, keyboard, or TV) are using SSH. If you have an SSH daemon running on your Raspberry Pi and it's connected to the network, you can access it through SSH using your host machine, with a command similar to this:

```
$ ssh root@192.168.1.13
root@raspberrypi2:~#
```

Now we are ready to get going with connecting the relay and lamp to our Raspberry Pi.

# Controlling the relay using the Raspberry Pi

To start with, we will control only the relay from the Raspberry Pi connected to it. This will be done using GPIO pins. First, we need to connect the relay to our Raspberry Pi in the correct way. The following table shows the connection scheme:

| Wire (color) | GPIO pin | Relay pin |
|---|---|---|
| Red | 3.3V (pin 1) | Power/VCC (+) |
| Black | GND (pin 6) | GND (-) |
| Yellow | GPIO 17 (pin 11) | IN (Signal/S) |

When this scheme is physically applied, it will look like the following figure. Remember that the exact order of the relay pins might look different between different models.

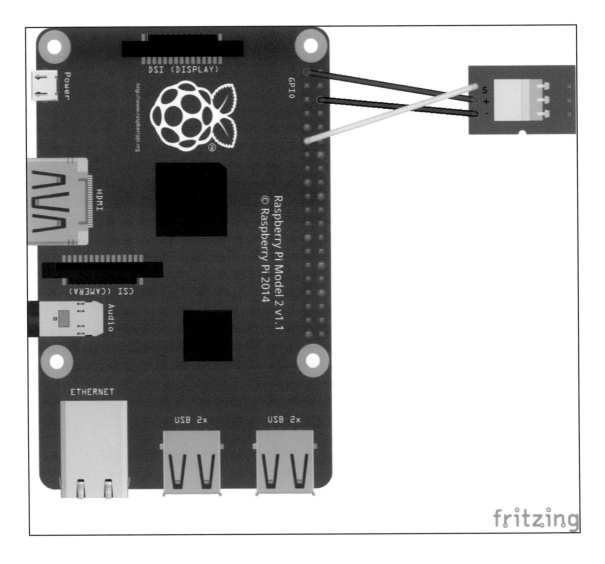

A Raspberry Pi 2 connected to a one-channel relay module, using GPIO 17 for the signaling

When the connection to the relay is complete, we can continue with next step: turning on or off the small LED connected to the relay. Most relays have a small LED attached to them. If your relay doesn't have an LED indicator, don't worry; we will look at some methods of checking from the command line whether the GPIO pin is active or not. There exist a number of different methods to control the GPIO pins on the Raspberry Pi; in this book, we will learn how to use sysfs and **RPi.GPIO** to control the GPIO pins.

We will start by learning how to use sysfs to turn the LED on and off. First, we need to export the GPIO pins and thereby make them visible from the userspace:

```
$ echo 17 > /sys/class/gpio/export
```

Next, we can see that a `gpio17` directory with some files has popped up in `/sys/class/gpio`:

```
$ ls /sys/class/gpio17/
```

After that, we need to set the direction (in/out) for the GPIO pin; in our example, we want the GPIO to act as an output pin:

```
$ echo "out" > /sys/class/gpio/gpio17/direction
```

Finally, we can enable the GPIO pin, which will cause the LED to turn on, by writing 1 to the `value` file:

```
$ echo 1 > /sys/class/gpio/gpio17/value
```

To turn off the light, we can write to the `value` file:

```
$ echo 0 > /sys/class/gpio/gpio17/value
```

When done, you need to `unexport` the GPIO pin:

```
$ echo 17 > /sys/class/gpio/unexport
```

Now, the `gpio17` directory in sysfs is gone. In our project, we will not manipulate the sysfs structure by hand. Instead, we will use the `gpio-packt` recipe added to our image earlier in this chapter, but under the hood, it uses the sysfs structure in a similar way as just described. The `gpio-packt` recipe produces a binary called `gpio_example`; it can be used to control GPIO17 using the following syntax:

```
$ gpio_example --led=1
$ gpio_example --led=0
```

Another way of controlling the GPIO pins is by using `RPi.GPIO`, which is a Python module that uses direct register access in the background to access GPIO. Controlling GPIO17 using RPi.GPIO requires that you add the following to a file called, for example, `ledon.py`:

```
import RPi.GPIO as GPIO
GPIO.setmode(GPIO.BCM)
GPIO.setup(17, GPIO.OUT)
GPIO.output(17, 1)
```

Then, we can run the script. Turning off the pin can easily be done by replacing `1` with in the `GPIO.output()` function:

```
$ python ledon.py
```

RPi.GPIO can also use the physical GPIO header pin numbering. In that case, GPIO17 will be placed on pin 11. To use this mode, the script must be modified as follows:

```
import RPi.GPIO as GPIO
GPIO.setmode(GPIO.BOARD)
GPIO.setup(12, GPIO.OUT)
GPIO.output(11, 1)
```

 The GPIO header diagram from `Chapter 8`, *Diving into the Raspberry Pis Peripherals and Yocto Recipes* can be used as a reference for understanding and playing with the GPIO pins.

# Controlling the lamp using the Raspberry Pi

At this point, we can control the relay locally from our board. Next, it's time to connect the lamp to our relay module.

WARNING: This project require basic knowledge of electricals. We strongly discourage using high-voltage power if you don't have the knowledge or experience. The recommendation is to use a low-voltage 12-V power supply.

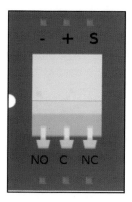

A one-channel relay module

Before we connect the lamp, we need to go through some basics about how the relay module will be used. Look closely at the following relay; it contains **C**, **NC**, and **NO** openings on the opposite side to where we inserted the GPIO jumper cables. These slots will be used to connect the lamp to the relay.

The **C** on the relay stands for common connection, and we will connect the power from our external power supply to this port. Next, we have **NC** and **NO**, which stand for **normally closed** and **normally open**. In our project, we will be using **NO**. The reason for this is that it will work like a switch. By default, there will be no contact between C and NO, but when we trigger the relay using the signaling from our GPIO pin, we will turn off the relay and that will open the circuit. Using NC instead of NO will give you the opposite behavior.

The lamp and the external power supply (12V strongly preferred for safety reasons) will be connected as shown in the following figure. Note that if no adapter is used for the lamp, you might need to open the outer shell of the cable to get the positive and negative wires. The black negative cable can be connected right from the external power supply to the lamp. The positive must be inserted from the power supply to the C slot on the relay. Finally, we need to connect the red positive cable from the lamp to the NO slot in the relay to get the required behavior as described earlier.

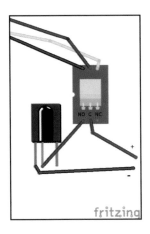

When all the physical connections are in place, we can check whether everything works by using the `gpio_example` binary again. At this point, our Raspberry Pi is probably hard to move, so we will use SSH to gain access to the board and turn the light on and off.

```
$ ssh root@192.168.x.x
root@raspberrypi2:~#
root@raspberrypi2:~# gpio_example --led=1
root@raspberrypi2:~# gpio_example --led=0
```

If everything has been set up in the correct way, you should see the light go on and off. In the next subsection, we will continue with controlling the light remotely by using a smartphone.

# Turning on/off the lamp from a smartphone

Our home automation project is nearly finished, but one important thing remains: we need to ensure that it's possible to control the light using a remote device, such as a smartphone. First of all, we need to check on the board whether the web server is present:

```
$ ps | grep server
295 root 2732 server.init
```

If the server for some reason hasn't auto-started, we can try to manually start it using this command:

```
$ /etc/init.d/server-packt-init start
starting Nodejs app: server.init... done.
root@raspberrypi2:~#    info  - socket.io started
listening on *:3344
```

If we manually perform some changes to the web server directly on the Raspberry Pi, we can restart the web server by using this command:

```
$ /etc/init.d/packt-server restart
stopping Nodejs app: server.init... stopped node (pid 295)
done.
starting Nodejs app: server.init... done.
```

Now, we can start the web browser on our smartphone and go to `http://my_rpi_ipaddress:3344`. You will see the same page that we saw when we opened `index.html` earlier in the chapter. The format might look a little bit different on a smartphone, but the red and green buttons will be there! Try tapping them and you will see the light go on and off.

A real-world example of the final result of the home automation project.

At this point, your home automation project is up and running, and you have managed to get one step closer to a wirelessly connected home. Hopefully, this project will give you plenty of ideas of how to set up other fun and creative home automation projects using a Raspberry Pi.

# Extra – using a Raspberry Pi with an LCD as the client

We can easily use an additional Raspberry Pi for the client side, which will be responsible for turn the lamp on and off. For this example, we will use the tiny PiTFT 2.8 touchscreen to control the light. Note that other touchscreens, of course, will work just as well; the important thing is that the image contains a web browser:

```
$ source /path/to/poky/oe-init-build-env pitft28r_client_proj
```

Update `bblayers.conf` like this:

```
$ cat local/bblayers.conf
# LAYER_CONF_VERSION is increased each time build/conf/bblayers.conf
# changes incompatibly
LCONF_VERSION = "6"
BBPATH = "${TOPDIR}"
BBFILES ?= ""
BBLAYERS ?= " \
        /path/to/poky/meta \
        /path/to/poky/meta-yocto \
        /path/to/poky/meta-yocto-bsp \
        /path/to/meta-raspberrypi \
        /path/to/meta-openembedded/meta-oe \
        /path/to/meta-openembedded/meta-multimedia \
        "
BBLAYERS_NON_REMOVABLE ?= " \
        /path/to/poky/meta \
        /path/to/poky/meta-yocto \
```

Then, update local.conf:

```
$ echo "MACHINE = "raspberrypi2"" >> conf/local.conf
$ echo "MACHINE_FEATURES += "pitft pitft28r"" >> conf/local.conf
$ echo "LICENSE_FLAGS_WHITELIST = "commercial"" >> conf/local.conf
```

 NOTE: This example uses the raspberrypi2 image; if you have a different model, remember to change it to the correct machine name.

Build the image with the following command, boot it, and go to `http://my_rpi_ipadress:3344`:

```
$ bitbake core-image-sato
```

# Summary

In this final chapter of the book, we repeated the techniques we learned throughout the book. This was done by creating a home automation project, which can wirelessly turn on and off lamps in your home with help from a Raspberry Pi and a web browser, using your smartphone as the remote, for example.

For our home automation project, we improved some of the examples used earlier in the book, such as the GPIO control binary and the Node.js examples. By evolving them, we revised how to modify existing recipes by appending them with new files or patching the old ones. The project also required you to revise how to create and integrate external layers. Further on, the chapter looked closer at some techniques and introduced you the usage of a specific package list in your project and how to use a serial connection and SSH to easily access and debug your Raspberry Pi. In order to complete the project, you were required to learn more deeply how the GPIO header and pins for the Raspberry Pi models are set up.

Using the skills learned in this chapter will hopefully inspire you when developing new cool and crazy home automation projects for the Raspberry Pi platform.

# Index

## A

Angstrom
  about 12
  URL 12
application
  developing 69, 70, 71
  developing and using, on LCD display 141
  recipe explanation 72, 73, 74
  recipe, creating 71, 72

## B

base, setting up for home automation project
  image recipe, customizing 167
  image, booting 168, 169, 170, 171
  image, building 168, 169, 170, 171
  new layer, creating 167
  setting up 167
BBLAYERS variable 25
bblayers.conf file
  editing 26, 27
Bitbake tasks
  about 53
  do_compile 54
  do_configure 54
  do_fetch 53
  do_install 54
  do_package 54
  do_patch 54
  do_unpack 53
BitBake
  about 12, 47
  user manual 47, 48
  working 13
Buildroot
  about 9
  reference, for documentation 9

URL 8

## C

canutils
  reference 50
class files 48
con2fbmap 162
configuration files 48
core components, Yocto Project
  about 10
  BitBake 12
  metadata 16
  OpenEmbedded-Core 14
  Poky 11
cross-compilation 58
  about 61
  compilation 62
  list of tools 62
  SDK environment configuration 61
custom application
  developing, Qt used 142, 143, 144, 145
customized package list
  setting up 178
  using, in meta-packt-iot 179

## D

DEB package format 64
dependencies, BitBake 50, 51
developing kernel 128
development environment, Yocto Project
  Application development SDK 18
  build system 18
  images 18
  metadata layers 17
  package feeds 18
  source files 17

user configuration 17
device tree (DT) 134
device tree blobs (DTBs) 134
device tree source (DTS) 134

# E

environment variables 25
external layers
  adding, to Raspberry Pi 82

# F

fbset tool
  about 162
  reference 162
fetcher backend
  about 51
  Git fetcher 52
  HTTP fetcher 52
  local file fetcher 51
fragments 132
Fritzing
  URL 69

# G

general purpose input output (GPIO) pins 69
Git fetcher 52
git scm
  reference 23
Git tool 21
Git
  about 148, 149
  workflow 149
  working with 149, 150, 151, 152, 153, 154
gpio-packt
  adding, to meta-packt_rpi 88, 89, 90
  patch, adding to recipe file 90, 92
  patch, generating 90
  patching 90

# H

Hob
  about 33
  environment, preparing 33
  image, building 42, 43, 44

packages, configuring 40, 41
recipes, configuring 40, 41
running 34, 36, 38, 39
home automation project
  base, setting up 167
  building 180
  creating 165
  lamp, controlling with Raspberry Pi 186, 187, 188
  lamp, turning on/off from smartphone 189, 190
  materials required 166
  packet list, creating for image 178
  Raspberry Pi used 165, 166
  relay, controlling with Raspberry Pi 183, 184, 185, 186
  serial and SSH connections, to Raspberry Pi 180, 181, 182, 183
  server side, creating 171, 172, 173, 174, 175, 176, 178
HTTP fetcher 52

# I

i2c bus 103, 104
i2c protocol 103
i2c-tools 109
i2cdetect 109
index.html 116, 117
IPK package format 65
IPK packages
  about 68
  automatic installation 68, 69
  manual installation 68

# J

jethro 137

# K

kernel configuration, with LCD support
  about 133
  Raspberry Pi device tree 134
  touchscreen, configuring from kernel perspective 135, 136
kernel releases
  reference 128

kernel.org  129

# L

layers
  about  75, 76
  distribution  77
  machine (BSP)  77
  miscellaneous  77
  reference  76
  software layer  77
  theory  76
LCD display, setting up for Raspberry Pi
  PiTFT 2.8 resistive touchscreen  139, 140, 141
  Raspberry Pi 7 touchscreen  137, 138, 139
  Yocto Project used  137
Linux distributions
  reference  20
Linux kernel
  about  127, 128
  configuring, in Yocto  132, 133
  configuring, with LCD support  133
  getting started process  129, 130, 131
  versus Raspberry Pi Linux kernel  128
local file fetcher  51
local.conf file
  editing  26
localmaster  154
longterm kernel  128
LTIB
  URL  8

# M

machine (BSP) layer  80, 82
main application, web interface project
  creating  116
  server.js  117
mainline kernel  128
maintainer  148
meta-oe layer
  inclusion, to SPI bus  99, 100
meta-packt_rpi layer
  creating, with yocto-layer script  85, 86, 87, 88
  gpio-packt, adding to  88, 89, 90
meta-qt5 external layer  142
meta-raspberrypi  16

  contributing to  156, 157
  Git repository, setting up  157
meta-string  86
meta-toolchain recipe  59
meta-toolchain-qt toolchain  60
meta-toolchain-qt5  61
meta-webserver
  reference  82
metadata, BitBake
  about  48
  classes  48
  configuration  48
  parsing  49
  recipes  49
metadata
  about  16
  meta-yocto  16
  meta-yocto-bsp  16
mkknlimg tool  134
Monkey
  URL  82
MOSI  97

# N

Nunchuck protocol
  about  107
  encryption  108
  sensor data, requesting  108

# O

OE-Core  8, 22
oe-init-build-env script  25
open source  147
open source projects
  contributing to  148
OpenEmbedded-Core
  about  14
  organization  15
OpenWRT
  URL  8

# P

package formats
  about  63

DEB 63
IPK 64
RPM 63
selecting 64, 65
package manager
  about 63
  package formats 63
package revision (PR) server 169
package
  installing, on target 65
  updating, on target 65
pitft 140
pitft28r 140
Poky 11
Poky image
  available images, listing 27, 28
  BitBake, running 29, 30
  booting, on Raspberry Pi 31
  building 27
  SD card, creating 30
Poky metadata
  downloading 21, 22
Poky on Fedora 21
Poky on Ubuntu 20
preferences, BitBake 50
providers, BitBake 50

## Q

qmake 143
Qt SDK 60
Qt5 SDK 61

## R

Raspberry Pi BSP metadata
  downloading 22, 23, 24, 25
Raspberry Pi connection
  about 107
  i2c connection, testing 109, 110
  integrating, with meta-packt_rpi 110
  Nunchuck application, creating 110
  Nunchuck application, testing 112
  Nunchuck protocol 107
  Nunchuck recipe, creating 111
  V4L presentation 112
  v4l-utils integration 113

video support 112
Raspberry Pi Linux kernel
  about 128
  reference 128
Raspberry Pi
  and package manager 63
  spi-config 101, 102
  spi-pipe 102, 103
  testing 101
  using, with LCD as client 190, 191
raspberry-packt-image.bb image
  creating 92
  deploying 95
  environment, creating 92
  recipe file, modifying 93, 94
  reference 95
recipes 49
remote branches 153
remote origin 154
required packages, for host system
  bblayers.conf file, editing 26, 27
  installing 19
  local.conf file, editing 26
  oe-init-build-env script 25
  Poky metadata, downloading 21, 22
  Poky on Fedora 21
  Poky on Ubuntu 20
  Raspberry Pi BSP metadata, downloading 22,
    23, 24, 25
rpi-basic-image 37, 168, 171
RPi.GPIO 185
RPM package format 64
RPM packages
  about 65
  automatic installation 65, 66, 67
  manual installation 65

## S

SCLK 97
sendmail tool 147
Serial Peripheral Interface (SPI) protocol 97
server.js file 116, 117
software development kits (SDKs)
  about 57
  generic SDK 59

image.bb -c populate_sdk  59
Qt SDK  60, 61
Qt5 SDK  61
software layer
  about  78
  classes folder  79
  conf folder  79
  COPYING  79
  README  78
  recipes-* directory  80
SPI bus
  about  97, 98
  conclusion  103
  inclusion, into meta-oe layer  99, 100
  Raspberry Pi, testing  101
  spi-tools project  98
  spi-tools, baking  100
SPI protocol
  reference  98
spi-tools project
  about  98
  spi-config  99
  spi-pipe  99
SRC_URI parameter
  reference  52
stable kernel  128
sysfs  185

**T**

tar.bz2 file
  reference  22
theory layer
  about  76
  name  76
  priority  76
Toaster
  about  44
  BitBake, running  45
  exploring  44
  required packages, installing for host system  44
  running  44, 45
  web interface, running  46
toolchain  57

**U**

Untracked files  150
upstream  148

**V**

V4L  112
vcgencmd command
  reference  117

**W**

web interface project
  about  115
  application, testing  125
  CPU temperature monitoring  115
  future  126
  hardware/software requisites  116
  main application, creating  116
  overview  116
  raspberry-packt-image, deploying  124
  Yocto/OE environment, creating  118
Wii Nunchuck
  about  105
  Nunchuck connector  106
working branch  153

**Y**

Yocto Project Manual
  reference  60
Yocto Project
  about  7, 8
  build system  8
  changes, sending to community  160, 161
  commit, creating  158, 160
  contributing to  155, 156
  core components  10
  custom tool upstream, sending  162, 163, 164
  follow-up  161
  practical example  162
  workflow  17
yocto-layer  167
yocto-layer script
  meta-packt_rpi layer  87
  used, for creating meta-packt_rpi layer  85, 86, 88

Yocto/OE  57, 58
Yocto/OE environment, web interface project
  creating  118
  image, modifying  118

init file, autostarting  121, 122, 123
recipe file, autostarting  123, 124
recipe file, creating  118, 119, 120
Yocto/OpenEmbedded
  URL  8

Made in the USA
Lexington, KY
29 December 2016